## Table of Contents

Preface..................................................................................................................................2

Introduction to Libra ..........................................................................................................3

Libra's Essentials.................................................................................................................6

Libra vs Banking system....................................................................................................12

The threat to the Global Economy ...................................................................................15

Actions being taken by governments ...............................................................................17

Altcoin Problem Statement ..............................................................................................19

Altcoins: History and Introduction ...................................................................................20

Altcoins and the Cryptocurrency Ecosystem ...................................................................21

Common questions regarding Cryptocurrency .................................................................23

Why Cryptocurrencies Work? ...........................................................................................27

What's Different in Trading Crypto Assets ........................................................................31

How to trade with Cryptocurrencies? ..............................................................................33

A Couple of Altcoins in detail ...........................................................................................35

Connection between Bitcoins and Altcoins.......................................................................38

Crytocurrency Mining........................................................................................................42

Bitcoin as a Global Reserve Currency ...............................................................................48

Digital Currency Wallet......................................................................................................52

ICO Regulatory and Reporting Framework........................................................................56

Blockchain Ecosystem........................................................................................................63

The Economy of Bermuda .................................................................................................70

Conclusion and a Vision for the Future .............................................................................76

# Preface

Numerous nations in the World have demonstrated to be prolific ground for the advancement of digital forms of money and blockchain advances. The rise of these advances is part of a more extensive influx of advances that encourage shared (P2P) trade, the individualization of items, and the flexibilization of creative strategies.

For a number of reasons, these patterns picked up footing after the worldwide monetary emergency a decade back. Blockchain advances intend to sort out P2P exchanges and P2P information streams without middle people and national banks have chances to utilize blockchain innovations to improve their administrations.

It is hazy how these advancements will create over the long haul; their definitive effect might be altogether different from the present applications. Accordingly, arrangement producers ought to strike a harmony between controlling the promotion encompassing these new advances and unleashing conceivably transformational new chances. While empowering and facilitating these advancements, they ought to get ready to make new guidelines to make a level playing field for new and old ventures, by altering money related oversight, shopper assurance, what's more, charge organization. They should likewise address the gigantic volume of power utilized to mine digital forms of money.

There are a number of digital currencies which people are using today as an alternative to paper currency, some of them have been around for a considerably long time such as the Bitcoin, some are new which encompasses most of the Altcoins and some are just announced yet an have made many heads turn. Yes, you guessed it right I will tell you all you need about the talk of the town which is Libra, facebook's own cryptocurrency which is to be announced in the early part of 2020.

After reading this book you will know quite some things about these digital currencies and have a clearer mindset whether you should invest in them or just stay away from them.

# Introduction to Libra

### History of Libra

Facebook VP David A. Marcus moved from Facebook Messenger to another blockchain division in May 2018. First reports of Facebook arranging digital money, with Marcus in control, rose a couple of days after the fact. By February 2019, over 50 designers were taking a shot at the task.

Affirmation that Facebook proposed cryptographic money previously developed in May 2019. As of now, it was known as "GlobalCoin" or "Facebook Coin".

Libra was officially reported on June 18, 2019. A first form is anticipated to be discharged in 2020.

Libra is a consent blockchain advanced money proposed by the American internet-based life aggregate Facebook. The undertaking, cash, and exchanges are to be overseen and depended on the Libra Association, an enrollment association established by Facebook's auxiliary Calibra and 27 others crosswise over installment, innovation, media transmission, online commercial center, funding, and charities.

As of June 2019, the money and system don't yet exist, and the main simple exploratory code has been discharged. The dispatch is wanted to be in 2020.

The whitepaper subtleties the present issues confronting worldwide funds, including constrained access for specific people and high expenses. The paper additionally calls attention to a couple of challenges, for example, the absence of reception just as instability shown by digital money resources.

In the whitepaper, the Libra has credited three key parts:

"It is based on a safe, adaptable, and solid blockchain [... ] It is sponsored by a save of benefits intended to give it natural worth, and it is administered by the autonomous Libra Association entrusted with advancing the environment." Facebook's advantage keeps running on an open-source blockchain called the Libra blockchain, and works in connection to hold, the whitepaper noted.

"Libra is completely upheld by a hold of genuine resources. A container of bank stores and momentary government protections will be held in the Libra Reserve for each Libra that is made, building trust in its inborn worth. The Libra Reserve will be directed with the target of protecting the estimation of Libra after some time."

The benefit will be a stable coin of sorts, the whitepaper expressed. "Libra is intended to be a stable advanced digital money that will be completely upheld by a save of genuine resources — the Libra Reserve — and bolstered by a focused system of trades purchasing and selling Libra." The Libra Association will be responsible for the coin supply and its connection to the hold.

## What is Libra?

Gossipy tidbits have been coursing about cryptographic money created or potentially overseen by Facebook for in any event a year, and now it is at last out in the open for individuals to find as Libra. Libra is a digital currency overseen by the Libra Association that enables clients to trade fiat money for Libra (for example purchase and sell Libra) for use in online exchanges. To drive the broadest reception, Libra does not expect clients to have a financial balance or a credit extension, for example, a charge card to possess any Libra cryptographic money — they essentially need to change over cash into or out of Libra to utilize it.

The Libra Association, the controlling hand for the youngster digital money, is comprised of accomplice organizations. The most prominent members are installment processors like Visa, Mastercard, and PayPal. Together, these accomplices guarantee that installment handling is quick, exact, and dependable with the goal that exchanges are as frictionless as could reasonably be expected.

## How does Libra work?

There are a couple of segments that make Libra what it is, yet the principal ones are the job of the Libra Association and the Libra save. The Libra Association is in charge of running the validator hubs, the figuring server groups that procedure exchanges, and, like this, are the main ones permitted to include or expel Libra from the course. At dispatch, the affiliation will run 100 of these hubs, yet the number will increment as scaling requires, and as more accomplices join.

This arrangement recognizes Libra from most different cryptographic forms of money. While increasingly normal cryptographic forms of money like Bitcoin are decentralized and task the person with keeping up the worldwide record by "mining" coins (for example performing cryptographically unquestionable "evidence of-work" calculations), Libra is concentrated and registered completely by the Libra validator hubs. To keep up exactness and counteract twofold spend assaults, the Libra validator hubs utilize a framework known as Byzantine adaptation to non-critical failure, in which hubs can figure out how to achieve an accord (for this situation, on the territory of Libra executed) notwithstanding when the hubs can't all concede to the condition of different hubs. In particular, it utilizes a variation of the HotStuff Byzantine adaptation to an internal failure convention named LibraBFT, which can oblige disappointment or obscure states by up to 33% of all validator hubs.

The other significant piece to Libra is its hold. Many decentralized digital currencies, remarkably Bitcoin, experience the ill effects of unstable valuation. While this can demonstrate rewarding for high-chance speculation purposes, Facebook tried to make an increasingly steady digital money to support it as a method for encouraging customary online purchaser exchanges. Libra does this by sponsoring all its issued computerized cash by a hold. Establishing Members are required to pool cash into the hold, with the possibility of arrival on their speculation utilizing profits from a low-yield venture of the save's benefits. You can likewise add to the hold when they trade fiat cash for Libra. By pegging Libra to officially sanctioned cash, the thought is that worth will remain moderately steady.

## Would we be able to confide in it?

Facebook has been tormented with outrages and information ruptures over the recent years, making some legitimately questionable about the protection of this money related administrations. That being stated, Libra has some significant security that includes set up to ensure your cash.

The stage is modified in Rust, which is, for the most part, viewed as great at taking care of memory, and the keen contract component is written in Libra's very own Move language, which makes careful arrangements to limit how information can be moved. Albeit Byzantine adaptation to internal failure is viewed as the hardest class of foundational disappointments to tackle in figuring, the HotStuff convention has noteworthy qualities in its detail.

As far as protection, it is indistinct how well the stage will deal with it. Libra's site demands that "The affiliation itself isn't engaged with handling exchanges and does not store any close to home information of Libra clients," however they are in charge of running the validator hubs, which will be involved with your information. They additionally demand that they will help the law requirement, which would not be conceivable except if they held some measure of client information. Regardless of whether validator hub administrators did not share information among themselves (past what is vital for finishing client exchanges, clearly), there could be issues. On the off chance that this stage is genuinely worldwide, as Libra means, even the part of the traffic that one hub would be handle could be worthwhile for information adaptation purposes, particularly with the system beginning at just 100 hubs.

The Libra site additionally guarantees that "exchanges don't contain connections to a client's genuine personality." This likewise appears to be difficult to accept. The entire reason for how cryptographic forms of money capacity is that any spectator can check where assets have gone, a capacity which Libra has saved notwithstanding its brought together design. Regardless of whether this case is valid, personal conduct standards can undoubtedly recognize clients without unequivocal characters.

The declaration from Facebook expressed that "Calibra won't share account data or money related information with Facebook or any outsider without client assent. This implies Calibra clients' record data and budgetary information won't be utilized to improve promotion focusing on the Facebook group of items." It ought to be focused on that you actually "assent" when you consent to the arcane client understandings that accompany any application or stage, so this isn't generally a substantive confirmation from Facebook. Also, second, even though Libra may well discount advertisement deals, the information could be offered to money related organizations for use in deciding financial assessments, for example.

Considering Facebook's not exactly sterling record on client security, you are all in all correct to be suspicious of Libra's protection claims. The open-source codebase, in any case, could help lighten concerns, accepting it is appropriately reviewed by unbiased outsider onlookers and made available.

# Libra's Essentials

### Budgetary sources of Libra

The arrangement is for the Libra token to be upheld by budgetary resources, for example, a bushel of monetary standards, and US Treasury protections trying to stay away from instability. Facebook has reported that every one of the accomplices will infuse an underlying US$10 million, so Libra has full resource backing on the day it opens.

Libra administration accomplices, inside the Libra Association, will make new Libra cash units dependent on interest. Libra cash units will be resigned as they are reclaimed for customary money.

The beginning compromise of exchanges will be performed at each administration accomplice, and the blockchain's disseminated record will be utilized for a compromise between administration accomplices. The aim is to help counteract everybody except individuals from the Libra Association from attempting to remove and dissect information from the disseminated record.

Rather than digital forms of money, for example, bitcoin which utilizes permissionless blockchains, Libra isn't decentralized, depending on trust in the Libra Association as "a truly national bank".

### Blockchain accord

Libra won't depend on digital money mining. Just individuals from the Libra Association will most likely procedure exchanges using the authorization blockchain.

Libra wants to change to a permissionless verification of-stake framework inside five years; even though their materials concede that no arrangement exists "that can convey the scale, steadiness, and security expected to help millions of individuals and exchanges over the globe through a permissionless system."

The move is the Libra blockchain's proposed keen contract and custom exchange language. It is wanted to be a statically-composed programming language, aggregated to bytecode. The venture gives this case of a Move shared exchange content in the Move white paper.

A center fundamental of Bitcoin from its initiation has been that it's decentralized. Nobody association or individual can change Bitcoin exchanges, nor would they be able to adjust wallets or square anybody from utilizing it. That is because the Bitcoin blockchain is completely decentralized, with a huge number of hubs spread everywhere throughout the world approving exchanges. There is no essential to turn into a hub, put something aside for having the PC equipment required to store the blockchain and a system association with an update it.

To change the Bitcoin blockchain you would need to control over 51% of all the registering power on the blockchain. Considering whole datacenters of explicit Bitcoin mining gear exist everywhere throughout the world, you'd need billions of dollars worth of registering hardware to try and attempt.

Libra is obviously logically focused. While it isn't actually as controlled as something can envision Ripple and its XRP token, Libra will be directed by the Libra Association, a social affair of associations from an arrangement of ventures, who will all have a state in its consistent improvement and undertaking. They've paid $10 million a piece to be there and Facebook has said that they'll all get a vote in issues identifying with Libra's improvement. It plans to have 100 people before the year's finished.

Those individuals can likewise run hubs in the event that they wish, however, to begin with, Facebook is relied upon to run most of them. That implies that with a straightforward vote, the individuals from the affiliation could square exchanges, change the blockchain, or even stop it briefly on the off chance that they picked up a larger part inside the Association.

That is extraordinary for blocking crime on the Libra arrange and could help return any stolen Libra to the first proprietor, yet it gives Facebook and the Association far more noteworthy controls over the digital money than anything any Bitcoin hub can have.

### Programming

Libra's source code is written in Rust and distributed as open source under the Apache License with the dispatch on 18 June 2019.

Elaine Ou, a sentiment essayist at Bloomberg News, took a stab at accumulating and running the openly discharged code for Libra. As provided, the product did minimal more than enable phony coins to be placed in a wallet; practically the majority of the white paper usefulness isn't executed, including "major engineering highlights that presently can't seem to be imagined." Ou was astounded that Facebook "would discharge programming in such a state."

### Guideline

Bitcoin is exceptionally difficult to direct. Organizations and governments could make the in and exit ramps for Bitcoin venture and divestment troublesome, yet as long as hubs exist someplace on the planet, Bitcoin can be executed. It could be exchanged for money, for merchandise, administrations, and all way of wares that aren't held by unified financial associations. It would be for all intents and purposes difficult to prevent Bitcoin from being utilized completely or to try and direct it successfully.

Libra, then again, caused a tremendous blend in worldwide governments the day it was reported and its white paper uncovered. Albeit no guidelines have yet been set on it, governments are now quick to explore it and have cautioned they may direct it later on. There may likewise be endeavors at tax assessment, if conceivable.

Since Libra is a generally brought together digital money, it's superbly practical to control in these habits. While it would, in any case, be an innovative obstacle, governments can toss their weight against Facebook on the off chance that they don't care for what's going on. Not so with Bitcoin.

### Advanced Wallet

Facebook plans to discharge an advanced wallet called Calibra in 2020, made accessible in Messenger, WhatsApp, just as in an independent application.

### What's its value

Nobody very realizes what Libra will be worth at this time. It could be a billion dollars for each token, or a few pennies. It doesn't especially make a difference until it begins to be dispersed, yet when it becomes open, the worth ought to remain moderately consistent. Like fiat monetary forms, Libra will be sponsored by something to help keep its incentive from being excessively unpredictable. Facebook has picked a choice of true monetary standards to put together Libra's an incentive with respect to, so regardless of whether one accident, it shouldn't take Libra excessively far with it.

There has been some worry over which monetary forms will be picked, notwithstanding, and whether the expansion of new monetary forms as sponsorship, later on, could influence the cost of the tokens — bringing up issues over the monopolistic intensity of Facebook and the Libra Association.

In an examination, there is nothing backing Bitcoin other than what individuals are happy to pay for it. That is the reason it can experience such tremendous swings in the worth, and why the following splitting occasion in 2020 could cause such interruption as diggers briefly clutch their Bitcoin as opposed to selling, to help blow up the incentive to make the procedure gainful once more.

### Centralization

Bitcoin varies altogether from Facebook's new resource from multiple points of view. Maybe the most outstanding distinction lies in Bitcoin's decentralization. No single substance controls Bitcoin. Conversely, Facebook and the Libra Association have a lot of authority over the Libra resource and its utilization. The arrangement of Libra's Association likewise seems to give sizeable elements (or picked substances) control over what may turn into a top worldwide resource — the Libra. Bitcoin does not offer control to such organizations in a similar manner.

## Trust and protection

As much as some may tout Bitcoin as a private, mysterious digital money, it isn't. It's semi-unknown, with no real way to demonstrate somebody possesses an unaffiliated record or wallet, yet exchanges can be followed on the open blockchain. That is the reason those looking for additional protection and namelessness use tumblers to further muddle their actions. Altcoins like Monero offer significantly more better security for the protection seeker.

Libra, be that as it may, is obscure in this field. It's not yet certain whether exchanges can be freely followed, or whether that is something that just Facebook and the Association will approach. Facebook has expressed openly that it intends to separate church and state and keep the Facebook informal organization altogether separate from Libra, regardless of it going about as the principal stage for its utilization. In any case, with Facebook's rehashed security gaffs throughout the years and its regularly antagonistic position toward the holiness of individual information, there are worries that Facebook could use Libra buys and exchanges to advance its income from selling individual information of clients or to make notices significantly more focused on.

While Bitcoin probably won't be impeccable in its security insurances, its absence of a solitary purpose of oversight makes it far simpler to trust for some.

## Facebook's Libra Asset

Working under the name Libra, Facebook's advanced resource will be utilized for worldwide installments, as per its whitepaper discharged on June 18. "Libra's main goal is to empower straightforward worldwide cash and budgetary framework that enables billions of individuals," the whitepaper states.

The whitepaper subtleties the present issues confronting worldwide funds, including constrained access for specific people and high expenses. The paper additionally calls attention to a couple of challenges, for example, the absence of reception just as instability shown by digital money resources.

In the whitepaper, the Libra has credited three key parts:

"It is based on a safe, adaptable, and solid blockchain [… ] It is sponsored by a save of benefits intended to give it natural worth, and it is administered by the autonomous Libra Association entrusted with advancing the environment."

Facebook's advantage keeps running on an open-source blockchain called the Libra blockchain, and works in connection to hold, the whitepaper noted.

"Libra is completely upheld by a hold of genuine resources. A container of bank stores and momentary government protections will be held in the Libra Reserve for each Libra that is made, building trust in its inborn worth. The Libra Reserve will be directed with the target of protecting the estimation of Libra after some time."

The benefit will be a stable coin of sorts, the whitepaper expressed. "Libra is intended to be a stable advanced digital money that will be completely upheld by a save of genuine resources — the Libra Reserve — and bolstered by a focused system of trades purchasing and selling Libra." The Libra Association will be responsible for the coin supply and its connection to the hold.

As indicated by the whitepaper, "The Libra Association is an autonomous, not-revenue driven enrollment association headquartered in Geneva, Switzerland. The affiliation's motivation is to facilitate and give a system to the administration for the system and hold and lead social effect award making in the help of monetary incorporation. The affiliation's enrollment is framed from the system of validator hubs that work the Libra Blockchain."

Included different organizations, associations, and foundations situated over the globe, the Libra Association's rundown of "Establishing Members" is very significant. The rundown incorporates any semblance of PayPal, Mastercard, eBay, Lyft, Vodafone Group, Coinbase, Andreessen Horowitz and Union Square Ventures. The advantage is relied upon to dispatch inside the initial a half year of 2020, the whitepaper noted.

The Libra will start as a permission blockchain, with the objective of turning into a permissionless system, the whitepaper said. Libra's blockchain additionally varies from customary blockchain innovation with respect to its chain: "The Libra Blockchain is a solitary information structure that records the historical backdrop of exchanges and states after some time."

Facebook is getting into the cryptographic money advertise. It declared a computerized wallet called Calibra on Tuesday, which it intends to dispatch in 2020.

The organization needs to be the one to bring the revealed 1.7 billion "unbanked" grown-ups into the universe of budgetary administrations under its umbrella. Be that as it may, the organization's answer isn't another Bitcoin — a long way from it. Libra, as the cash is known, is intended to permit Facebook clients to make buys on the informal organization and different sites on the web.

Instead of a decentralized token, like Bitcoin, Libra will be overseen and constrained by Facebook and a consortium of organizations like Visa and Mastercard. You'd be on the right track to figure it doesn't sound much like your run of the mill cryptocurrency. In any case, with Facebook's stage available to its, does Libra have the energy to be the primary digital currency made for the majority?

**Incorporated digital money**

Libra has been a work in progress for over a year on Facebook. Before distributing a white paper in mid-June, the person to person communication monster looked for and keeps on looking for, financing from organizations to help create Libra and award them access to the consortium of firms that will oversee it pushing ahead. These establishing individuals from the "Libra Association," have just been joined by significant stages like Booking.com, and Argentina-based internet business website, MercadoLibre, just as Uber, Visa, Mastercard, and PayPal. Those are some enormous players in the advanced financial world.

The declaration has some cryptographic money devotees revving their motors, making some enormous cases on Libra. The potential is positively there. Facebook's colossal impact in informing and long range interpersonal communication give it a span and straightforward entry that few organizations could want to contend with. Be that as it may, Bitcoin fans are probably not going to be as awed. Libra isn't Bitcoin, regardless of whether it shares the equivalent basic blockchain innovation and is based upon likewise open source programming. It's the nearest agent inside the current crypto-space is Ripple and its XRP token, however that brought together digital currency still isn't exactly what Libra is. Libra is progressively similar to Disney Dollars for an online environment like Facebook.

Even though not as unified as Ripple with a solitary organization controlling its future, Libra is as yet set to be overseen by a gathering of huge money related and innovative associations, just as financial speculators, telecoms, and scholarly foundations. Some of which will control the on exit ramps for a venture. That goes against the thought behind generally cryptographic forms of money.

Take Bitcoin, for instance. It's extraordinarily difficult to direct and control by its very structure. It's decentralized with nobody element ready to apply command over its blockchain, or the exchanges that happen on it. Libra is depicted as a "permission" arrange, which approves hubs and right now, requires budgetary speculation from them, to be considered.

Where Bitcoin was intended to expel the guardians from the money related world, Libra just makes Facebook and its affiliation the main watchmen that issue. Their aggregate power makes them the main ones who can mint new Libra tokens, or consume (pulverize) existing ones. With a 66% lion's share of affiliation individuals casting a ballot on it, they could even hypothetically lock individuals out of their Libra wallets, or square exchanges from occurring altogether.

With Bitcoin and most different cryptographic forms of money, none of that is conceivable. Nobody can control the cash that goes into or out of Bitcoin. That is one of its actual qualities, but at the same time is one reason it's confronted trouble with selection on a mass-showcase scale. That likely won't be an issue for Libra, yet it raises inquiries regarding the fairness of the affiliation and its individuals.

Facebook and monetary supporters like PayPal, Visa, and Mastercard will have a stake and a state in Libra's continuous advancement and however the white paper claims that the arrangement is to make Libra permissionless later on, there's no assurance of that. The investigation into it isn't planned to start for an additional five years after the dispatch one year from now, so it's very conceivable such charitable points will be unobtrusively disregarded. There's surely nothing halting new individuals from the relationship with fundamentally various thoughts regarding its activity from influencing that 66% casting a ballot lion's share later on.

## Libra vs Banking system

Purchasers will presumably view holding Facebook's new cash, Libra, as an option in contrast to placing cash in the bank. On the off chance that they consider it to be an appealing option, Libras could multiply. On the off chance that each Westerner held in Libra a sum equivalent to one-tenth of their bank stores today, the new money remarkable would be worth over $2trn. How stressed should banks be?

At first pass, Libra resembles a financial arrangement of sorts. The "Libra Reserve" will hold enough fluid safe resources for back each Libra it issues. A staunch minority of financial analysts has for a considerable length of time required this kind of course of action —named "limited banking" — to supplant the current "fragmentary save" model, under which stores at banks are sponsored by home loans and other illiquid advances. Thin banks, they contend, would not endure runs. Superficially, the main evident contrast between the Libra Reserve and a restricted bank is that the previous will hold resources named in an assortment of (still-to-be-indicated) monetary forms.

Facebook's digital money Libra professes to take care of an extremely critical issue: helping individuals without access to banks. I have my questions about how accommodating Libra will be.

As per the white paper, the whole purpose of Libra is to "empower basic worldwide cash and budgetary framework that enables billions of individuals." The organization claims Libra will help give individuals access to a less expensive arrangement of cash moves. Facebook refers to a measurement of 1.7 billion individuals overall who don't approach budgetary foundations, a measurement that begins with the World Bank's Global index Database 2017. Of these individuals, around 1 billion have cell phones and 500 million have web get to. Bits of knowledge like these have prompted the telephone installment framework M-Pesa, which as of now works in over 10 nations and does not utilize cryptographic money.

How about we begin with the undeniable missing measurement: we don't have the foggiest idea what number of individuals have Facebook accounts however no financial balances.

Half of all grown-ups who don't have ledgers are living in only seven nations; in four of those nations, it's difficult to perceive how Libra gets off the ground

As indicated by the report Facebook refers to, half of all grown-ups who don't have financial balances are living in only seven nations: Bangladesh, China, India,

Indonesia, Mexico, Nigeria, and Pakistan. In four of these nations, it's difficult to perceive how Libra gets off the ground.

Facebook is prohibited in China. A few nations, for example, Pakistan, Indonesia, and Bangladesh have briefly restricted Facebook for timeframes, conceivably constraining the adequacy of any cash attached to the application. Facebook makes reference to this as a hazard factor to its business in its quarterly recording: "Government experts in different nations may look to confine client access to our items in the event that they believe us to be infringing upon their laws or a risk to open security or for different reasons, and sure of our items have been limited by governments in different nations now and then."

That is not every: a large number of these nations have laws around cryptographic money. (Indeed, I know it is easily proven wrong whether Libra qualifies as cryptographic money or not. Be that as it may, Facebook is considering Libra digital money, so I will expect cryptographic money laws will apply.) India's present guidelines mean Libra can't work in the nation. Pakistan is thinking about guidelines for digital forms of money, however, at present, they are prohibited. Digital currency is likewise verifiably restricted in Bangladesh and China.

The huge success here is perhaps Indonesia, which just sanctioned exchanging digital currencies, and was likewise called out by Facebook in its latest quarterly documenting as a territory of developing day by day dynamic clients.

Yet, most of these nations have generous obstacles for Libra selection. This may clarify why Libra's establishing accomplices aren't situated in any of these nations. (MercadoPago, an online installment organization that is additionally one of the accomplices, operates in Latin America and is situated in Argentina.) No establishing Libra accomplices have all the earmarks of being situated in Asia or Africa, either — and that is the place the general population without financial balances are, as indicated by the World Bank details. It isn't difficult to see something like Libra took up, however, it will need nearby help; most nations have a brush of guidelines around banking. It doesn't look like Libra has called any nearby help yet in the spots it makes a difference most.

The white paper contains some detail on Libra's engineering. In any case, there's little exchange of why individuals don't have financial balances. As indicated by the World Bank information Facebook is referring to, just about 66% of individuals who don't have financial balances state this is because they don't have enough cash to open one. Libra does not tackle that issue. 33% of individuals who don't have financial balances said they needn't bother with one. No requirement for Libra there, either.

**Libra comprehends just the less mainstream reasons individuals don't have financial balances.**

Libra comprehends just the less mainstream reasons individuals don't have financial balances. About a fourth of respondents said banks' high and unforeseen charges were in any event part of why they didn't have accounts; separation to a bank was a boundary for another 20 percent. So these individuals would appear to be Libra's intended interest group.

There's kind of an unobtrusive hitch here, however: to utilize Libra, you need to purchase Libra. I'm not the first to see it; the Financial Times' Brendan Greeley has expounded on a similar issue. The papers themselves appear to believe their end client to be somebody like me, a woman with a financial balance and a charge card. The way toward changing over to Libra is depicted practically how I would encounter it: you sign on and give them your Mastercard number or ledger number.

The issue is, individuals who don't have banks don't have financial balance numbers and they might not have charge cards, either. They have money. "There's nothing about how Libra will lower charges to change over fiat money into Libra cash, which is both the basic test of purchaser banking and an express piece of Libra's concern proclamation," Greeley composes. "Registration spots charge ghastly expenses, yet they're ready, on interest, to transform physical looks into physical money, and physical money into exchanges."

Concerning portable banking, take-up has been interwoven. M-Pesa has been fruitful in Kenya. Be that as it may, in Nigeria, individuals still lean toward money since they stress if their telephones are stolen, their cash will be gone, as well. This is an issue of social standards, not a building. Conflicts among telecoms and banks hamstrung portable financial applications in Nigeria. This, as well, isn't an issue you can unravel through the building. There are other, progressively unremarkable issues with regards to portable banking also, similar to the expense of having inert clients.

## Libra doesn't address the fundamental issue the documentation says it's embarking to address

It's uncertain to me why a versatile installment administration like the one Facebook is proposing requires cryptographic money by any means. It appears like a non-starter in huge numbers of the business sectors where portable installments may be generally required. What's more, Libra doesn't address the primary issue the documentation says it's embarking to address.

From the documentation Facebook has given, a sensible individual may infer that the issue proclamation exists altogether as a smoke screen. Libra isn't intended for individuals without financial balances; it's intended for individuals who as of now have cash. Facebook is a business; organizations need to profit; as we have seen, individuals without financial balances generally don't have cash.

There's one more crimp in the documentation, which Coindesk's Ian Allison first detected: "An extra objective of the affiliation is to create and advance an open personality standard. We accept that decentralized and versatile advanced personality is essential to money related incorporation and rivalry." If Facebook's concern explanation is a trick, at that point the compact computerized character is another conceivable end game.

See, it's fine that Facebook is building a cash application for the advantaged class. That is ordinary Facebook! Yet, I don't trust Facebook is doing this for more noteworthy benefit. Perusing the documentation, it's difficult to get away from the end that all Facebook is doing is attempting to concoct another approach to line its very own pockets — regardless of whether that is Libra or an open character standard. Or on the other hand, you know, both.

## The threat to the Global Economy

Facebook's arrangement to work its computerized cash poses dangers to the Global financial framework that should trigger a rapid reaction from worldwide policymakers, as per the association that speaks to the world's national banks.

Despite the fact that the move of huge tech firms, for example, Facebook, Amazon, and Alibaba into money-related administrations could accelerate exchanges and cut expenses, particularly in creating world nations, it could likewise undermine the dependability of a financial framework that has just barely recouped from the accident of 2008.

Reverberating admonitions from numerous tech specialists, the Bank for International Settlements (BIS) said that while there were potential advantages to be made, the appropriation of advanced monetary forms outside the current money related framework could decrease rivalry and make information security issues.

"The point should be to respond to enormous authorities' passage into cash related organizations to benefit by the increases while compelling the threats," said Hyun Song Shin, financial guide and head of research at BIS.

"Open strategy needs to expand on a progressively complete methodology that draws on money-related guidelines, rivalry approach, and information security guidelines."

The notice from the BIS on Sunday comes just days after Facebook declared it would dispatch its own computerized money, Libra, in 2020. It will enable its billions of clients to make monetary exchanges over the globe in a move that could conceivably shake up the world's financial framework.

Chris Hughes, a prime supporter of Facebook, a week ago added his voice to concerns being communicated over enormous tech's move into money, cautioning that Libra could move influence into the off-base hands.

Hughes, who is co-seat of the Economic Security Project, an enemy of neediness crusade gathering, stated: "If even unassumingly fruitful, Libra would hand over a significant part of the control of financial approach from national banks to these privately owned businesses. If worldwide controllers don't act now, it could very before long be past the point of no return."

Shin said policymakers expected to think about whether the present framework, which enables banks to energize more and fabricate stores to ensure themselves amid an emergency, was desirable over an increasingly aggressive framework where exchange expenses were lower however the strength of the budgetary framework was less notable.

The draw of a more noteworthy challenge between adversary advanced monetary standards could demonstrate fanciful if a task like Facebook's Libra wound up overwhelming over the world.

He said policymakers likewise expected to organize their endeavors to ensure the new frameworks were directed to secure clients and anticipate them encouraging illegal tax avoidance.

Striking an increasingly positive note, the Bank of England a week ago mindfully respected the approach of computerized monetary standards, saying it would not build up its own but rather depend on the tight guidelines of private part activities.

Other tech organizations entering the fund world incorporate Alibaba and eBay, offering installment administrations Alipay and PayPal separately. Some enormous specialists have begun to offer protection items, utilizing their stages as a dispersion channel for outsider items, including vehicle and medical coverage. Others have wandered into loans, for the most part to littler organizations and customers, regularly loaning limited quantities for brief periods.

For the most part, huge specialists have made more prominent advances where the arrangement of installments is constrained and cell phone infiltration high. For example, as an enormous portion of the populace in developing business sector economies remains unbanked, the high cell phone proprietorship rate has permitted computerized conveyance of fundamental budgetary administrations, including cashless installments, to beforehand unbanked family units and little and medium-sized undertakings.

Advances have been primarily in China yet besides growing quickly in south-east Asia, East Africa, and Latin America. Money related administrations are as yet a little piece of huge tech business, speaking to about 11% of incomes over an example of enormous tech organizations.

BIS said that the new participants to the market could have an upper hand over banks and serve firms and family units that generally would remain unbanked however controllers would need to guarantee a level playing field between enormous tech organizations — which have a wide client base and access to data — and banks.

Given the activities of huge specialists straddle distinctive administrative edges and geological outskirts, coordination among national and worldwide experts will be pivotal, BIS said.

# Actions being taken by governments

### Why Facebook's Libra cash gets the disapproval

The sparse data gave about the purpose, jobs, potential use, and security of the Libra and Calibra uncovered the enormous size of the dangers and the absence of clear administrative insurances. On the off chance that items and administrations like these are left inappropriately controlled and without adequate oversight, they could present foundational dangers that imperil the US and worldwide money related steadiness.

These dangers are significant in light of Facebook's recent history, where it didn't generally protect its clients' data. For instance, Cambridge Analytica, a political counseling firm employed by the 2016 Trump crusade, approached over 50 million Facebook clients' private information which is utilized to impact casting ballot conduct.

Maxine Waters, the seat of the house board of trustees on monetary administrations, has been one of the main congressional Democrats requiring the reprimand of Donald Trump. "90% of the calls and mail I'm accepting in my office bolster indictment of Trump thus do I," she wrote in April.

### Libra: US Congress asks Facebook to delay development

Lawmakers state they need time to research cryptographic money and its potential effect. The US Congress has asked Facebook to stop the advancement of its Libra cryptographic money until administrators have had more opportunity to research the repercussions of the organization's activities.

In a letter from the Democratic leaders of the House panel on money-related administrations and its subcommittees, the administrators ask the organization to "promptly stop execution plans".

"Since Facebook is as of now in the hands of over a fourth of the total populace, it is basic that Facebook and its accomplices promptly stop execution plans until controllers and Congress have a chance to look at these issues and make a move," the letter says.

"During this ban, we mean to hold formal reviews on the dangers and advantages of digital money based exercises and investigate authoritative arrangements. Inability to stop usage before we can do as such dangers another Swiss-based budgetary framework that is too huge to come up short."

Although Facebook has initiated the improvement of Libra and will make the main buyer "wallet" for the money through its Calibra auxiliary, the real advancement of the administration will be given over to the Libra Association, an association headquartered in Geneva, Switzerland.

The affiliation is run ostensibly by a consortium of Libra's underlying supporters, including Visa, Lyft, Vodafone and Coinbase, of which Facebook is only one accomplice among many. In any case, by and by, the interpersonal organization holds a lot of control, notwithstanding paying the pay rates of the body's "generally about six representatives", as indicated by the business news site the Information. The span of the ban on advancement need not be that long: the congressional board of trustees is meeting a full hearing inspecting Libra on 17 July. Be that as it may, the letter, which was conveyed to Mark Zuckerberg, Sheryl Sandberg, and Libra's CEO, David Marcus, recommends the organization is in for a rough ride when the consultation happens.

### Facebook cautioned by UK financial regulators Libra digital currency will go under examination

UK money related controller features worries over customer insurance and security Facebook's arrangements for a worldwide digital currency, Libra, will warrant examination by governments over the world, as indicated by one of the UK's most senior money related controllers.

Christopher Woolard, the official executive of procedure and rivalry at the UK's Financial Conduct Authority (FCA) featured a progression of potential issues with the computerized money, from customer assurance and protection worries to budgetary market steadiness.

Facebook would like to take off Libra in June 2020, permitting more than 2bn month to month clients worldwide to complete monetary exchanges utilizing the stage without precedent for immediate danger to the current financial framework.

Talking at a gathering in Cambridge, Woolard stated: "Its size and scale will suggest conversation starters for society and government all the more for the most part about what is satisfactory and alluring in this space."

Randal Quarles, the leader of the Financial Stability Board, a week ago said that increasingly far-reaching a selection of digital forms of money would require the consideration of the worldwide administrative body.

The risk to money related security presented by Libra will most likely go under specific investigation given the high instability in the costs of different cryptographic forms of money.

The cost of bitcoin, the first digital money that advanced decentralized record innovation, has varied fiercely as of late after Facebook's Libra declaration.

The cost of one bitcoin fell underneath $10,000 (£7,900) at focuses on Tuesday, well beneath a month ago's the pinnacle of $13,880. As of late as March, it was exchanging underneath $4,000.

The FCA and different controllers have met Facebook agents to examine the plans, however experts still have a wide assortment of inquiries concerning the legitimate and handy subtleties of Libra.

# Altcoin Problem Statement

The appearance of the web and versatile broadband has enabled billions of individuals universally to approach the world's learning and data, high-loyalty correspondences, and a wide scope of lower-cost, progressively advantageous administrations. These administrations are currently available utilizing a $40 cell phone from anyplace in the world.1 This network has driven monetary strengthening by empowering more individuals to get to the money related biological system. Cooperating, innovation organizations, and money related foundations have additionally discovered answers for assistance increment financial strengthening the world over. In spite of this advancement, huge swaths of the total populace are still deserted — 1.7 billion grown-ups universally stay outside of the money related framework with no entrance to a customary bank, despite the fact that one billion have a cell phone and almost a large portion of a billion have web access as well.

For too much, portions of the money related framework look like media transmission systems pre-web. Twenty years back, the normal cost to send an instant message in Europe was 16 pennies for every message. Now everybody with a cell phone can convey over the world for nothing with an essential information plan. In those days, broadcast communications costs were high yet uniform; while today, access to budgetary administrations is constrained or limited for the individuals who need it most — those affected by cost, unwavering quality, and the capacity to consistently send cash.

Everywhere throughout the world, individuals with less cash pay more for budgetary administrations. Hard-earned pay is disintegrated by expenses, from settlements and wire expenses to overdraft and ATM charges. Payday advances can charge annualized loan fees of 400 percent or more, and money charges can be as high as $30 just to obtain $100.4 When individuals are inquired as to why they stay on the edge of the current budgetary framework, the individuals who remain "unbanked" point to not having adequate assets, high and eccentric expenses, banks being excessively far away, and coming up short on the fundamental documentation.5

Blockchains and digital currencies have various interesting properties that can conceivably address a portion of the issues of openness and reliability. These incorporate circulated administration, which guarantees that no single substance controls the system; open access, which enables anyone with a web association with taking an interest; and security through cryptography, which ensures the uprightness of assets.

Be that as it may, the current blockchain frameworks still can't seem to achieve standard selection. Mass-advertise utilization of existing blockchains and cryptographic forms of money has been ruined by their instability and absence of versatility, which has, up until this point, made them poor stores of significant worth and mechanisms of trade. A few activities have additionally planned to disturb the current framework and sidestep guideline rather than enhancing consistency and administrative fronts to improve the viability of hostile to illegal tax avoidance. We accept that working together and improving with the monetary segment, including controllers and specialists over an assortment of ventures, is the best way to guarantee that a reasonable, secure and believed structure supports this new framework. What's more, this methodology can convey a monster jump forward toward a lower-cost, increasingly available, progressively associated worldwide money related framework.

## Altcoins: History and Introduction

Each altcoin needs some sort of story to tell. On the off chance that an altcoin can't guarantee some trademark that recognizes it from all the others, there is no explanation behind it to exist. In the least difficult case, an altcoin changes a portion of the implicit parameters to Bitcoin. These parameters incorporate, for instance, the normal time between obstructs, the square size point of confinement, the timetable of remunerations being made, and the expansion rate of the altcoin. There can likewise be progressively mind-boggling specialized contrasts, which makes the altcoin additionally intriguing. For instance, increases in the scripting language can express various types of exchanges or security properties. Mining could work quickly, and the accord calculation could be altogether not the same as Bitcoin's. At times altcoins are propelled with a subject or a feeling of a network that the altcoin is planned to help or be related with, frequently giving individuals from this network a unique job or capacities in the altcoin. We take a gander at instances of these conceivable outcomes later in this segment.

Bitcoin was launched in Jan 2009. It wasn't for one more two years, till the center of 2011, that the primary Bitcoin-like derived system, Namecoin, was launched. the speed of altcoin launches exploded in 2013, and a whole bunch has since up. variety} are there in all? a precise number is not possible to calculate, as a result of it's not clear that altcoins are price tally. for instance, if somebody annonces an altcoin and maybe releases some ASCII text file, however, nobody has started mining or victimization it, however, will that count? different altcoins are launched and seen some initial use, then again died quickly once their launch. It's additionally approximately clear what's Associate in Nursing altcoin, as opposition merely another cryptanalytic currency. After all, there have been numerous cryptocurrency proposals and systems that predated Bitcoin, and that they are typically not referred to as "altcoins." several altcoins borrow ideas from Bitcoin, usually directly forking its code base or otherwise adopting a number of its code. Some create solely minor modifications to Bitcoin, like ever-changing the worth of some parameters of the system, and still incorporate changes created by Bitcoin's developers. To date, all altcoins that we all know of beginning with a brand new genesis block and their own alternate read of dealings history, instead of forking Bitcoin's blockchain once an explicit purpose in history. For our functions, we tend to don't would like a definite definition of an altcoin. Instead, we'll loosely see a cryptocurrency launched since Bitcoin as an altcoin. Here we tend to mention en passant non-altcoin systems like Ripple and Stellar: These are distributed accord protocols within the tradition thought-about in identifiers and wish to remember of 1 another. Bitcoin, of course, radically departs from this model. In each Ripple and Stellar, the accord protocol supports a payment/settlement network, and every system contains a native currency. Despite these similarities with altcoins, we tend to don't think about them too.

# Altcoins and the Cryptocurrency Ecosystem

Bitcoin is only one segment (though a significant one) of a more extensive biological system of option, yet regularly very comparative, monetary forms called altcoins In this section, we take a gander at altcoins and the environment of digital currencies.

### Deciding the Value of Money

The estimation of a nation's cash is presently best characterized using its conversion scale versus another nation's money. The US dollar remains the world's hold currency and it is consequently the principle pair member for practically all monetary forms, a position that rose as a major aspect of Bretton Woods. For example, it is normal for two non-USD monetary forms to be previously matched against the USD to encourage a non-USD cross-cash exchange. Regarding how those qualities are resolved, monetary forms right now openly skim, are fixed to another money, or then again utilize a crossover of a free and fixed model, frequently called an oversaw or filthy buoy.

The vast majority of the world's biggest economies enable their monetary forms to uninhibitedly coast, with China's overseen buoy being an eminent special case. Under an openly skimming cash routine, valuation is controlled by money free market activity factors, which causes trade rates to always vary. A worldwide remote trade market is evaluated to exchange $5.3 trillion in monetary standards every day and works 24 hours out of every day on each weekday. The advantage of having a profound and every now and again exchanging business sector is that valuations mirror all current data and value change can, for the most part, keep away from enormous market stuns in everything except outrageous conditions.

The cost of cash in the outside trade (FX) markets are resolved by the hidden interest made by universal exchange alongside the speculative angles made by dealers hoping to benefit from value variances. Fare of products and enterprises makes the clearest wellspring of interest, as a

provider will by and large wish to be paid in their neighborhood money. In oversimplified terms, the shipper would need to procure the outside money by selling their nearby money to make the installment for those products and enterprises. This makes interest for an exporter's cash, driving its worth higher, while including supply (selling) of the other cash, driving its worth lower. In any case. History of Money reciprocal exchange may make a request on the two sides and if there is an equivalent trade of merchandise, the equalization of exchange is impartial and there will be no need for any change in FX rates from an exchange point of view.

In the real world, the adjusted exchange is an uncommon event, with nations running exchange shortages or surpluses, here and there in sizable amounts for expanded timeframes. Under a great highest quality level, changes in cash supply would be managed by the adjustments in gold saves because of deficiency and surplus adjusts. The adjustments in cash supply like this would grow or contract the particular economies, making times of more noteworthy riches in a single country over another. The better performing economy would probably devour more, while the residents of the shortfall country would discover their utilization abridged. A decent's costs and the request would, at last, be affected, as the net shippers come back to adjust through a mix of less expensive fares furthermore, fewer imports. All through this period, trade rates would be unaltered as they are fixed to the estimation of gold. Skimming monetary forms give a comparative change instrument, even though the conversion scale itself adjusts the free market activity condition. In our oversimplified model gave over, the nation that is a net shipper runs an exchange deficit, while the fare driven nation has an exchange overflow.

Concentrating on the deficit nation, the estimation of its cash decays as there is less interest concerning the surplus nation (as inferred by their exchange circumstance). The decrease in cash esteem, at last, makes its merchandise less expensive to the outside world, which in the end brings the exchange unevenness over into equalization. The inverse is valid for the surplus nation as its more grounded cash currently makes its products progressively costly and consequently less alluring. It would see its fares along these lines fall, adding to make the move unbiased. At last, rising or then again falling fares sway the abundance of a country's residents, which has clear political repercussions that make our straightforward model simply hypothetical and not especially helpful for deciding the estimation of cash in reality.

# Common questions regarding Cryptocurrency

### What is cryptographic money?

At first, hailed as a defiant innovation that would overturn the world's money related foundations and free individuals from the burdensome charges and controls of the financial foundation, the digital currency has since been discolored by crime and wild market theory. And keeping in mind that everybody has known about crypto names like Bitcoin, not many individuals comprehend the basics of how digital forms of money really work — particularly with regards to the individual fund. This is what you have to know to keep you from getting ripped off, and furthermore help you decide whether digital forms of money are for you.

Cryptographic money is fundamentally an advanced method to hold and move esteem on the web. You can buy digital money tokens or coins on the web (with a Visa or "customary" cash), and there is ordinarily nobody individual or bank that controls specific cryptographic money. There are many diverse digital forms of money accessible on the web, the greatest and most understood ones being Bitcoin or Ethereum.

The estimation of any digital money at some random time relies upon free market activity. There's generally a fixed measure of any cash accessible at some random minute, so the more individuals need to utilize it, the higher the cost. In late 2017, for instance, the cost of a solitary Bitcoin took off to generally $20,000 and after that took a drive to around $4,000.

### How would I spend cryptographic forms of money?

On the off chance that you have your very own wallet under your very own advanced lock and key, you can "send" individuals computerized reserves. To do this, the vast majority will in general utilize online vaults, similar to those given by Coinbase. The procedure is fundamentally the same as conventional online administrations: you essentially enter the measure of cash you need to send and the organization you need to pay.

A few sellers acknowledge digital currencies. Microsoft will give you a chance to add Bitcoin to your record web based utilizing your computerized wallet, for instance. What's more, there's a developing rundown of things you can buy with digital currency, including everything from compelling artwork to land. By and large, the reception of digital money installments has been to a greater extent an advertising move than a down to earth budgetary one, however it can give cryptographic money tokens greater steadiness.

On the drawback, you ought to know that a large portion of the outlets that acknowledge digital money additionally put huge confinements and impediments on it. In any case, most just acknowledge the main cryptographic forms of money, Bitcoin and Ethereum. Second, you will most likely be unable to utilize the credit for each administration. For instance, Microsoft will give you a chance to utilize Bitcoin to purchase diversions, films, and applications in Windows and Xbox stores — yet you can't utilize it in the Microsoft online store or purchase gift vouchers with it.

### Are there any concealed expenses?

There is a large portion of the autonomous and startup trades that will purchase and sell cryptographic forms of money for you additionally charge a type of expense for the administration. What's more, similar to genuine stock representatives, they make you come and go, at whatever point you purchase or sell cash.

### Is it secure?

That relies upon your point of view. The facts demonstrate that cryptographic forms of money that utilization blockchain innovation guarantee that exchanges are recorded appropriately and make it hard to hack. Blockchain programming is a decentralized record that no single individual or organization controls because the record of all exchanges are kept up over different hubs, offering excess and making it amazingly hard for any one client to mess with.

Notwithstanding, if a cryptographic money token is stolen from an advanced wallet, much of the time that implies the cash is away for good and untraceable. Besides, a few vaults have been hacked as much as of a few million dollars, again leaving clients with no response because the assets are not insured or guaranteed by any administration establishment (balance this with conventional ledgers in the US, which the FDIC conceals for to $200,000). A year ago, over $1 billion was stolen from cryptographic money trades.

## Is it true that it isn't only for hoodlums?

Generally, crypto was the domain of hoodlums and advanced theorists who were likely pulled in by the simplicity with which Bitcoin can be exchanged online without trading off namelessness. Individuals who traffic in stolen information and medications on the dull web were enormous starting advocates of digital currency. In any case, it has picked up authenticity in the course of recent years as a result of its adaptability for moving computerized cash online without the requirement for any type of institutional banking. It has likewise picked up support in nations like Venezuela where the nearby cash is insecure and subject to wild inflationary swings. In these circumstances, the digital currency can offer some security against political agitation.

## Is it superior to anything other online installment administrations?

In a word, no. The crucial issue with all digital forms of money is the eccentric change in their worth. So while you clutch a specific computerized section, you could be losing (or picking up) cash until you use it to purchase something or empty it. Conventional cash (what crypto advocates allude to as "fiat" money) will, in general, be progressively steady since it's upheld by governments and a lot bigger system of worldwide exchanging markets.

## Is it still a major ordeal?

Indeed and no. The theoretical air pocket of 2017 on the planet's most prominent digital money, Bitcoin, burst — yet Bitcoin is still broadly utilized. Individuals work together in Bitcoin in what might be compared to up to $800 million every day. That may sound like a great deal, however, it's not exactly 50% of what one customary administration, Paypal, does every day.

Be that as it may, it is picking up acknowledgment as a class of cash, to a great extent since privately owned businesses see huge promoting potential — and another wellspring of income — in propelling their cryptographic forms of money (see ICOs beneath).

## What are ICOs?

Beginning coin contributions (ICOs) are a route for organizations to fund-raise by issuing virtual tokens. Much like crowdfunding, you buy these virtual tokens utilizing customary cash or another digital currency like Bitcoin or Ether, and the organization as far as anyone knows utilizes it to make items and grow. It enables the organization to maintain a strategic distance from the lawful and money related necessities for raising funding or issuing stock. This new type of crowdfunding is overflowing with hazards, in any case.

For the most part, you can just utilize the tokens you purchase to buy administrations or items from that organization. So ICOs are useless anyplace else and there is dependably the threat that the organization will neglect to create anything worth purchasing — and there's no real way to recover your cash. Besides, ICOs have been issued in a few tricks, leaving purchasers between a rock and a hard place. Also, there's an impressive theoretical market too, with some auxiliary markets jumping up and dealers trading the tokens on the web and driving up their worth.

A turn off the idea from ICOs is for privately owned businesses to issue their cryptographic money to be utilized distinctly at its stores. It can likewise be utilized like extra miles or focuses, redeemable later on for the organization's administrations. One major player taking a shot at its digital money for online cash trades is Facebook. Be that as it may, its prosperity — like that of a wide range of cryptographic money — will rely upon how much individuals trust it.

# Why Cryptocurrencies Work?

Now that you know that compared to precious metals, paper currencies are not real money; it's time to divert our attention to cryptocurrencies as an alternative to paper currencies, because they're a lot nearer to gold than paper money as we all know it these days is, and why they'd work in far better manner than paper currencies.

### Low Risk of Disruption

According to David John Grundy, the worldwide blockchain head of one of the world's biggest banks, Danske Bank, the sole means anyone will stop or shut blockchains down is by taking down the web itself. And by now, I feel you recognize that's much not possible. It's like saying someone will keep the sun from shining or the wind from blowing, it sounds unnatural.

### Portability

Unlike edict currencies, cryptocurrencies may be simply transferred from one account to a different using on-line gadgets like computers, tablets or perhaps smartphones. With edict currencies, you'll need to do that therefore physically or through an equivalent bank. Plus, you don't need to bring them with you physically as a result of that they are safely stored on the internet. therefore you can go to any corner of the world with a decent internet connection and convey your cryptocurrencies with you no matter the amount!

### Better price Storage

You can solely think about as an asset as decent price storage if it's able to keep comparatively unchanged levels of utility or satisfaction over time. Applying this to monetary assets, it suggests that having the ability to keep up buying power over time. A monetary asset's ability to stay price may be estimated through what's referred to as elementary analysis, which takes into thought each the quantitative and qualitative aspects of such an asset that anyone owns.

The ability to keep the worth has become the first foundation for investment or holding cryptocurrencies like Bitcoin, Ethereum, and others. however will cryptocurrencies ever be able to keep their worth and if they will be, will they be doing it well?

## The Gold Comparison

Don't be stunned to find cryptocurrencies being compared to precious metals, i.e., Bitcoin to gold and Litecoin or Ether to silver once justifying cryptocurrencies' ability to store value over the future. one amongst the explanations - albeit a shallow one - is that the representation of cryptocurrencies. Bitcoins are visually shown as color gold whereas Litecoins are visually represented as silver. however, these simple visual cues justify the assumption in cryptocurrencies' ability to store values just like the 2 most precious metals on Earth. we tend to mustn't dismiss behavioral economic science that underlies all the asset categories. When a lot of folks begin believing that cryptocurrencies like Bitcoin, Ether, or Litecoin can hold their worth like precious metals like gold and silver will, it will push the costs of those cryptocurrencies upward. once their costs do go up over time, then it's extremely attainable that they'll be able to keep or maintain their values during an extended time.

Comparisons to precious metals, e.g., Bitcoins to gold, maybe a robust issue that may influence the direction of general markets concerning Bitcoin's and altcoin's skills to retain or keep their worth in the future. And this may have an enormous impact in terms of the number of investors who'll read cryptocurrencies normally pretty much as good investment vehicles.

## Limited amount

Just like gold in its physical type, cryptocurrencies like Bitcoin generally have a restricted amount of units, that is outlined or set in their several blockchain protocols. Bitcoin, for instance, has a total quantity of solely twenty-one million units that may ever be created. Litecoin on the opposite hand has a total 84-million unit cap that's controlled by its operative protocols. this is often what makes cryptocurrencies deflationary or disinflationary over a long time.

Remember our discussion earlier on provision and demand and the way the value of assets are change with changing market conditions? As a result of these cryptocurrencies have a set range of units that will ever be made, their supply relative to the number of products and services that could be bought with them in the future is effectively shrinking. meaning that their buying power may be expected to extend over the long haul and may have deflationary effects on merchandise and services.

## Independence from alternative quality categories

Compared to any or all alternative monetary assets such as real estate or paper currencies categories like stocks or paper currencies whose values fluctuate counting on the pronouncements or moves created by central bankers or monetary regulators, the actual worth of gold and silver can't be manipulated by any central financial authority no matter their macro-policy selections are. attributable to its autonomy from any monetary authority, precious metals like gold and silver can bear currency price movements or market change over time, which makes them superb and worthy in the future.

Cryptocurrencies are like gold therein they're usually redistributed and autonomous naturally. This means rather like gold, government selections or policy changes have a very little direct impact, if at all, on their long term worth or market value. The extent of decentralization and autonomy may be a hot discussion topic among cryptocurrency users and investors, wherever some favor the complete autonomy version whereas others feel lighter with some compromise, i.e., hybrid mixtures of some sort of governance (not from the government) and decentralization. In general, cryptocurrency governance models will vary greatly with some adopting a balanced power structure among its users once it involves major decisions to be made on one point whereas others select the benevolent absolutism model on the opposite hand. And in between the 2 are a varied alternative combination or hybrid models. however normally speaking, cryptocurrencies with additional decentralized systems might do far better risk management in terms of hedging against the chance of their values being influenced or tampered with by regulators and would be better protected against cost manipulation by the market giants or the governments.

## Underlying or Intrinsic Values

Assets that are thought of to be truly valuable and hold their worth have underlying characteristics that serve as foundations for their long term values. In layman's terms, such assets have intrinsic utility values, i.e., practical uses that provide them their values. Gold, for instance, is employed for producing jewelry and electronic components like semiconductors. Land or real estate's underlying price or utility is their capability for having structures engineered upon them and therefore the extent of business their areas get. When it involves underlying utility price, cryptocurrencies have plenty of potentials. Especially, cryptocurrencies hold an enormous promise in terms of fixing the means monetary transactions are done online, that embrace the enforcement of contracts, records keeping, and payments. because the use of cryptocurrencies like Bitcoin, Litecoin and Ether are increasing day by day in the markets, their underlying values increase even more and more, which may increase their values over the long haul.

## Impossible To make counterfeit

The blockchain technology could be a revolutionary one in terms of facilitating online transactions and data or record keeping. Being such, it's much not possible to supply counterfeit versions of it. And as blockchains still evolve, it becomes more and more by every passing day    - if such a term exists - to supply counterfeit cryptocurrencies that may be used for purchasing stuff.

## Impossible to regulate

Particularly for cryptocurrencies whose market capitalizations are already within the billions of dollars like Bitcoin and Ether, one would wish an enormous quantity of cash to get hold of enough units of such cryptocurrencies simply to be able to influence or manipulate their costs. When you take a glance at Bitcoin, for instance, whose average capitalization hovers somewhere around US$50 billion, one would wish a minimum of US$10 billion to manipulate by the act of supply and demand. though you're talking regarding Ether, whose average market cap is much smaller at around US$25 billion to US$30 billion, one would still need a very big capital to get a hold of these coins and manipulate the market.

## You don't need a big initial capital

Unlike stocks and alternative monetary assets that need comparatively high amounts of investment capital, cryptocurrencies have low barriers to entry. meaning even those that solely have relatively little amounts of cash to speculate will simply get in. As such, cryptocurrencies, in general, have the next range of investors investing in them to the point that it becomes practically not possible to control the market.

**Relative Security**

Lastly, cryptocurrencies are just not possible to steal unlike paper currency if you store your coins on the right kind of storage device which is secure for your coins. The right kind of storage, that I'll quote later. however, if you trust your coin exchange blindly and keep all your coins on the web then there is a very big risk of your coins being stolen and you would not be able to do anything about it once they are stolen. Therefore if you follow my recommendation shortly concerning storage of your Bitcoins or alternative cryptocurrencies, you'll virtually be able to store your coins in a way that they are no chances that someone can steal them from you.

**How Trading of Traditional Financial Protections Is Structured**

In the conventional monetary markets, financial specialists, for the most part, need to open a brokerage account with a firm that gives the administrations and the connection that the financial specialist wants. In the event that they need to just exchange stocks at the least cost, there is no absence of rebate dealers to pick among. A higher touch relationship may require a full-administration firm that has an admired name and notoriety that makes one agreeable. Every last one of these conventional organizations can, regardless, get to huge numbers of similar items, for example, stocks, at practically indistinguishable costs, regardless of where the underlying request starts.

There is a long history of best practices and guidelines in the financier world. For example, client records ought to be isolated from the firm account, which confines them from any budgetary issues at the financier firm. The breakdown of Lehman Brothers is a genuine model, where financier clients were not affected by the financier association's default and had nearly prompt access to their stocks and bonds. All money market funds are moreover guaranteed by the Securities Investors Protection Corporation (SIPC) that spreads their advantages when they have been abused, as a rule through burglary or misrepresentation by the financier firm. This protection needs to restore the full estimation of portfolio advantages for the speculator on the off chance that they are inside the SIPC rules.

# What's Different in Trading Crypto Assets

While these insurances and procedures are frequently underestimated for conventional money related ventures they can't be neglected when picking a crypto commercial center. Right off the bat, financial specialists must understand that a crypto trade is like the securities exchange. When you exchange on a crypto trade, you are taking the opposite side against counterparties at that particular trade at the predominant costs for the picked trade. Crypto trades have not yet created proficient exchanging linkages the manner in which conventional securities exchanges have. For stocks, Silk Road to Wall Street: Accepting Crypto Currency as a Tradable. At the point when costs fluctuate crosswise over trades, this makes an exchange opportunity where you could purchase a stock at the less expensive trade and at the same time sell it at the progressively costly scene. This would rapidly close the hole and the distinctions in costs for a similar resource would vanish. That isn't yet valid for crypto trades, where the overall market costs for a similar resource, state Bitcoin, could shift by a few rate focuses, which isn't an inconsequential measure of cash when valuations are high. The differences are to a great extent driven by fluctuating liquidity crosswise over trades with the bigger stages offering better value disclosure because of more prominent movement. At the minute, the main five trades for Bitcoin volume are bitfinex, bitflyer, bitstamp, Coinbase, and Kraken, even though these rundowns change frequently.

Given the borderless idea of digital currencies, it is nothing unexpected that the top five trade postings have addresses in four unique nations. Financial specialists ought to accept that most trades are just delicately controlled, so picking the right home is another significant choice. While we have recorded the largest trades there are innumerable other little trades that will tout lower expenses, more develop estimating, better exchanging chances, or any number of benefits. Be that as it may, if these trades are not situated in your nation of habitation, it might be hard to determine major issues, for example, hacking, which has demonstrated to be a progressing concern.

Outside trade of fiat monetary forms likewise represents a conceivable issue in crypto cash trades. While it might be an abomination to consider liquidating out into old paper cash, there are as yet relatively few proprietors that will take crypto for lease installments. Getting your crypto gains in your home cash may not be as straightforward if the trade is situated in a remote locale and executes for the most part in non-local money sets. The equivalent is valid in setting up an account, with each trade building up its subsidizing necessities. For the case, Coinbase will acknowledge charge cards, which numerous different trades will not. Others, including bitfinex up to this point, just acknowledged coin stores, so new brokers would initially need to get crypto from another trade and move those coins to their record.

When working out the jurisdictional issues, it is essential to choose an

trade that exchanges the crypto that you are keen on. While for all intents and purposes all trades will exchange Bitcoin and Ethereum, it's anything but a given that more up to date computerized monetary forms will be on all stages. While Ripple posted the most grounded gains in 2017, one of the biggest trades, Coinbase, did not offer to exchange it. Given that there appear to be many new monetary standards included every month, picking the right trade for your exchanging propensities is basic. The requirement for security is clear after the various hacks that have affected trades everywhere throughout the world. While Mt. Gox was ahead of schedule in the crypto life cycle, the equivalent can't be said for coin check, which lost $500 million worth of coins in mid-2018. There have been various little hacks, a large number of which brought about trade conclusion also, financial specialist misfortunes. Since there is no SIPC protection for crypto trades, finding a firm with a decent notoriety that keeps client resources disconnected goes far to abstain from being hacked. A considerable lot of the hacks have happened with hot wallets or coin stores that are associated with the web, making them powerless against assaults. Speculators ought to eventually take their coins disconnected and store them in cool wallets that are not associated with the web and might be on a capacity gadget that you convey with you.

# How to trade with Cryptocurrencies?

### Utilizing Wall Street for Crypto Investing

There are extra approaches to partake in digital currency exchanging without owning computerized coins legitimately. As referenced, the CBOE and CME both offer Bitcoin fates, which has seen a consistent increment in volumes, albeit little in respect to other increasingly settled budgetary contracts for loan fees, value lists, and gold. There are additionally a predetermined number of ETFs that hold different interests in real coins or fates contracts. There are likewise new ETFs that put resources into firms associated with blockchain innovation, in spite of the fact that their top property is in tech firms that have grasped the blockchains, for example, Microsoft, Overload, and NVIDIA. There will without a doubt be more ETFs that are destined to be presented in the coming year as intrigue stays high in the digital money space. The benefit of these items is their capacity to take advantage of existing brokerage accounts, despite the fact that it ought to be noticed that a few dealers confine get to these speculations.

**Risk Status**

In contrast to fiat cash, there is a fixed measure of bitcoin (21 million BTC once all have been mined) which gives it properties like that of wares, for example, gold. Subsequently, its rate of expansion can't be overseen by an administration (or another administering body) to expand/decline swelling, joblessness, or speculation/financial development like that of fiat money. Rather, its natural swelling is, it could be said, worked in by means of a mining procedure. The apparent store of estimation of bitcoin is the thing that varies against the estimation of fiat monetary standards. In different words, bitcoin's "future value" will remain exceedingly defenseless against theoretical assaults, awful press, security ruptures, misfortune, shot of enormous holders selling, guideline and expense treatment, and so forth.

until Bitcoin appropriation achieves an adequately minimum amount to withstand these vulnerabilities. With an advertise capitalization under $10 billion and numerous huge holders of bitcoin, the cost is substantially more helpless to unpredictability than equivalent resource classes, for example, gold. This instability may frighten off speculators who are not acclimated with less directed markets that don't have circuit breakers to prepare for huge intraday value swings.

This deterrent additionally covers the risk of the purported "whales" who hold incredibly huge sums of bitcoin exchanging enough bitcoin that it drives down the cost to a point that may compromise its presence as a store of significant worth.

**The most effective method to Launch an Altcoin**

Think about what's engaged with the way toward propelling an altcoin and what occurs after dispatch. As we referenced, making an altcoin includes making another reference customer, commonly by forking the current code base of some current, all the more entrenched altcoin, or of Bitcoin itself. The simple part is to include specialized highlights or changed parameters you think will work out well. Truth be told, there was at one time a site called "Coingen" that would mechanize this procedure for a little expense. It enabled you to indicate different parameters like the normal square time and the evidence of-work calculation you needed, notwithstanding a name for your altcoin, a three-letter cash code, and a logo. At that point at the snap of a catch, you'd download a fork of Bitcoin with the parameters you picked, and you (and others) could promptly begin running it. The crucial step is the bootstrapping reception of your altcoin. You can fork the source code and you can report it freely, however now, no one is utilizing your altcoin.

So it has no market esteem (since no one needs the coins) and no security (since there aren't excavators yet). In the long run, you'll need to pull in every one of these sorts of members to your altcoin economy to get it off the ground. These gatherings are significant and interrelated. The test of collecting them is practically equivalent to that associated with propelling some other stage and getting it embraced. On the other hand if you had to get another mobile network working framework or any state you would have to get clients for that, additionally you would also have to get gadget makers and application designing professionals and also there would have to be partners which will gather to make a working system. Drawing in excavators has extraordinary significance for cryptographic forms of money, because, without sufficient hash influence behind an altcoin, security may flop severely if twofold spending and forks are conceivable.

On the other hand if you had to get another mobile network working framework or any state you would have to get clients for that, additionally you would also have to get gadget makers and application designing professionals and also there would have to be partners which will gather to make a working system.

Indeed, your altcoin may be kept running over altogether. There is no basic formula for bootstrapping selection, yet all in all, excavators will come once they accept the mining rewards they could gain would merit the exertion. To energize them, numerous altcoins give early diggers more noteworthy prizes. Bitcoin spearheaded this methodology, yet some altcoins have adopted a progressively forceful strategy to compensating early diggers. Persuading a network of individuals that the altcoin is profitable is the most troublesome trap. Notwithstanding for Bitcoin, it's not clear precisely how this procedure was bootstrapped, as it depends on the Tinkerbell impact. Encouraging this conviction binds back to why altcoins need a decent story: to get off the ground, its locale must accept that the new altcoin will end up profitable (and accept that others will trust it is important, etc). Other significant components, as a rule, pursue diggers and early adopters. These incorporate having your altcoin recorded on trades and developing different sorts of the supporting framework, going from a backing establishment to devices for investigating the blockchain.

# A Couple of Altcoins in detail

Here we center around a couple of the most seasoned altcoins and concentrate their highlights in more detail.

## Namecoin

We've perceived how Bitcoin's square chain is a protected, worldwide database. When information has been kept in touch with it, this information is sealed, and its incorporation can be demonstrated until the end of time. Might we be able to change Bitcoin's plan to help other utilization of secure worldwide databases, for example, a naming framework?

We need a couple of standard procedures to make this database progressively valuable for concurrency applications. To start with, we consent to see information passages as name/esteem sets, with names being all inclusive one of a kind. This permits everybody to look into the worth mapped to a name, much the same as a hash table or a database with an essential key field. To authorize the worldwide uniqueness of names, if a name/esteem pair has a similar name as a past database passage, at that point we see it as an update to the worth instead of another section.

Second, we concur that solitary the client who at first made the passage for a the specific name is permitted to make updates to that name. We can undoubtedly

implement this by a partner each name with a Bitcoin address and requiring the update exchanges to be marked by the private key for that address. We could do this over Bitcoin, similarly as we could fabricate any overlay cash utilizing Bitcoin as an attach just log. In any case, it's less complex to do it in an altcoin, because we can take this current "man of honor's understanding" and compose it into the standards of the altcoin. These standards would at that point be sacred and upheld by the excavators, as opposed to requiring every client (i.e., full hub) to check the standards and autonomously choose what to do if they are abused. Done appropriately, this usage would even permit SPV-style proofs: a lightweight customer would most likely present an inquiry (i.e., a name) to a server running a full hub, and the server would restore a worth for that name, alongside a proof that the returned worth is in actuality the most recent update for that name in the database.

That is Namecoin more or less. It's a worldwide name/esteem store, where each a client can enlist at least one names (for an ostensible charge) and after that issue updates to the estimations of any of their names. Clients can likewise move control of their names to other people. Truth be told, you can make an exchange that moves your area to somebody, and in the meantime moves units of the Namecoin money from them to you. Since this is a solitary nuclear exchange, it's a protected method to offer your area to somebody you've never met and don't trust. Starting at now, Namecoin doesn't bolster secure lightweight customers, yet an augmentation that supports them has been proposed. Namecoin will likely give a decentralized variant of the Domain Name System (DNS), the names in the database being space names and the qualities being IP addresses. You can't utilize this as a matter of course with an the unmodified program, however, you can download a program module for, state, Firefox or Chrome that would enable you to type in a location like example.bit—any area name that closures in ".bit"— and it will turn upward the area in the Namecoin vault rather than the customary DNS. Namecoin is, in fact, fascinating, and it's likewise verifiably intriguing — it was in actuality the first altcoin to be propelled, in April 2011, somewhat more then 2 years after Bitcoin was propelled. About every single enrolled area are taken by "squatters," trusting (yet bombing up until this point) to sell their names for a benefit. Namecoin supporters will, in general, contend that the current DNS puts as well many commands over a basic part of the Internet under the control of a a single substance. This view is well known in the Bitcoin people group, as you can envision, however it doesn't look like standard clients are clamoring for an option to DNS, denying Namecoin of the executioner application it needs to appreciate noteworthy reception.

**Litecoin**

Litecoin was likewise propelled in 2011, at some point after Namecoin. Starting at now, Litecoin is the main altcoin as far as by and large prominence and client base. It is likewise the most broadly forked codebase. Truth be told, it has been forked a bigger number of times than Bitcoin itself. The fundamental specialized refinement among Litecoin and Bitcoin is that Litecoin highlights a memory-hard mining riddle (given script). At the point when Litecoin was propelled, Bitcoin mining was in the GPU time, thus the objective of Litecoin's utilization of a memory-hard mining confound was GPU obstruction. When it was propelled, you could in any case mine on Litecoin with a CPU, long after this had turned out to be useless for Bitcoin. However, since at that point, Litecoin hasn't prevailed with regards to opposing the change to GPU mining and at that point to ASICs. Every one of those mining changes took somewhat longer in Litecoin than in Bitcoin, yet it's uncertain whether this is on the grounds that Litecoin's riddle was really harder to actualize in equipment or basically on the grounds that Litecoin's lower conversion standard gave less motivation to do as such. Regardless, the exhibition upgrades of ASICs contrasted with CPU digging is generally comparable for Litecoin as they are for Bitcoin. In this sense, Litecoin flopped in its unique objective of making an increasingly decentralized framework by keeping up a network of CPU diggers. Be that as it may, significantly, this account still worked for bootstrapping Litecoin—it pulled in numerous adopters who wound up remaining even after the first reason fizzled. Litecoin has since unequivocally changed its account, expressing that its underlying assignment was more reasonable than Bitcoin's, on the grounds that it opposed ASICs for more. Litecoin additionally makes a couple of minor parameter changes: for instance, squares in Litecoin arrive multiple times quicker than in Bitcoin, every 2.5 minutes. Litecoin generally acquires however much from Bitcoin as could reasonably be expected. Truth be told, its advancement has pursued Bitcoin, so that as patches and enhancements have been made to Bitcoin, Litecoin has additionally embraced them.

**Dogecoin**

Dogecoin has maybe been the most bright of all altcoins to date. It was discharged in late 2013, and what recognizes it isn't essentially specialized (it is a nearby fork of Litecoin) yet rather a lot of networks esteems: tipping, liberality, and not paying attention to digital currency so. In fact, it is named after Doge, an entertaining Internet image including a linguistically tested Shiba Inu hound. The people group has had a few fascinating and fruitful promoting efforts, for example, supporting a NASCAR driver and putting Dogecoin logos all over his vehicle. They additionally raised more than $30,000 to help the Jamaica National Bobsled Team, with the goal that the group could travel what's more, content in the 2014 Winter Olympics. Amusingly, this intently reflects the plot to the 1990s motion picture Cool Runnings.

**Dogecoin Developers.**

The blend of the network's liberality, PR exercises, and the innate image estimation of Doge implied that Dogecoin wound up mainstream in 2014. It creates the impression that a considerable lot of the early adopters were new to digital forms of money before Dogecoin, giving another network to bootstrap the money's an incentive without offering a convincing story in terms of a bit of leeway over different monetary forms. Dogecoin demonstrated that bootstrapping can be effective with a nontechnical story. However, as numerous Internet marvels, the notoriety has not kept going, and Dogecoin's swapping scale has since failed.

# Connection between Bitcoins and Altcoins

We can utilize different measurements to get a feeling of the relative size or effect of diverse altcoins.

## Market Capitalization

Generally, showcase capitalization ("advertise top") is a basic technique for assessing the estimation of an open organization by increasing the cost of a share by the all-out number of offers remarkable. With regards to altcoins, this market top is regularly likewise used to assess the all-out estimation of the altcoin by increasing the cost of an individual unit of the altcoin (estimated, maybe, at the most well-known outsider trades) by the aggregate the number of units of money of the altcoin thought to be available for use. By this measurement, Bitcoin is by a wide margin the biggest—starting at 2015, it represents more than 90 percent of the general market top of all of the digital currencies joined. The overall positioning of the different altcoins will, in general, fluctuate very much a part, however, the fact is that most altcoins are relatively minor regarding money related worth.

It's significant not to peruse a lot into the market top. To begin with, it isn't fundamentally the amount it would cost for somebody to purchase up every one of the coins in course. That number may be higher or lower since enormous requests will move the cost of the money. Second, despite the fact that the count considers just the coins as of now available for use, we ought to anticipate that advertise members factor into the conversion scale the way that new coins will come into course later on, which further muddles the elucidation of the number. At last, we can't even precisely gauge the genuine number of coins at present available for use, in light of the fact that the proprietors of a few coins may have lost their private keys, and we have no real way to know what level of coins has been lost?

## Different Indicators

There are a few different markers we can take a gander at. Changes in an altcoin's conversion standard after some time gives us intimations about its wellbeing and tends to associate with changes in its hash rate over a prolonged stretch of time periods. Trade volume on different outsider trades is a proportion of movement and enthusiasm for the altcoin. Conversely, the volume of exchanges that have been made on the altcoin's square chain doesn't disclose to us much since it could basically be clients rearranging their very own coins around in their wallet, maybe even naturally. At last, we can likewise take a gander at what number of dealers and installment processors support the altcoin—just the most unmistakable monetary forms will, in general, be upheld by installment processors.

## Financial View of Bitcoin-Altcoin Interactions

The connection between Bitcoin and altcoins is confounded. In one sense, digital forms of money rival each other, on the grounds that they all offer an approach to make online installments. In case there are two standards, shows, or associations in the contention that is commonly corresponding with respect to what they offer, by then one of them will, when in doubt, come to order, in perspective on what business experts call "framework impacts."

For instance, Blu-beam and HD DVD were in the savage challenge in the mid-to-late 2000s to be the successor to the DVD position. Step by step, Blu-beam begun to turn out to be progressively famous, an enormous part on the grounds that the mainstream PlayStation 3 support worked as a Blu-beam player. This made Blu-beam a increasingly appealing configuration for film studios and this prevalence benefited from itself: as more motion pictures were discharged for Blu-beam, more purchasers purchased independently Blu-beam players, prompting more film discharges, etc. Thus, if your companions all have Blu-beam players, you'd need to get one yourself as opposed to an HD DVD player, since you'd almost certainly effectively swap motion pictures with them. In around 2 years, the HD DVD was an authentic commentary.

This line of thinking recommends that one cryptographic money—apparently Bitcoin, which is by a long shot the most prominent one today—will command, regardless of whether some successor frameworks could be ostensibly in fact prevalent. Yet that would be a distortion. Rivalry among cryptographic forms of money is not as unfriendly as the challenge between circle designs for at any rate two reasons.

To begin with, it's generally simple for clients to change over one digital currency into another, and for sellers to acknowledge more than one cryptographic money, which implies that numerous cryptographic forms of money can all the more effectively exist together and flourish. In financial aspects terms, cryptographic forms of money display moderately low exchanging expenses.

Contrast this circumstance with that for DVD players, where the vast majority truly try not to need two massive machines in their homes and can't change over their existing library of plates on the off chance that they change to a machine that plays the other group. Exchanging expenses are absolutely not zero for cryptographic forms of money. For model, clients may purchase equipment wallets that can't be overhauled. Yet, by furthermore, enormous, it's anything but difficult to change digital forms of money or to utilize more than one at the same time.

Second, as referenced prior, numerous altcoins have one of a kind highlights that furnish them with an unmistakable explanation behind existing. These altcoins shouldn't be seen as simple substitutes for Bitcoin; they might be symmetrical, or maybe indeed, even corresponding. Seen thusly, correlative altcoins really increment the helpfulness of Bitcoin instead of rival it. In the event that Namecoin succeeds, for instance, Bitcoin clients have one progressively helpful thing they can do with their bitcoins.

In any case, this image of glad collaboration is likewise a distortion. A few altcoins, like Litecoin, essentially attempt to accomplish similar usefulness as Bitcoin however in an alternate, maybe increasingly productive, way. Notwithstanding when new usefulness is being offered, regularly those utilization cases can in certainty be accomplished in Bitcoin itself, but in a less exquisite manner. Supporters of the do-it over Bitcoin model contend that having various altcoins isolates the hash control accessible and makes each moneyless secure.

Conversely, supporters of altcoins contend that these substitute monetary standards permit market powers to figure out which highlights merit having, which frameworks are in fact prevalent, etc. They further contend that having various altcoins limit the harm of a potential cataclysmic disappointment of anyone framework. They call attention to that Bitcoin engineers are profoundly chance loath, and that adding new highlights to Bitcoin through a delicate or a hard fork is moderate and troublesome. Conversely, it is anything but difficult to evaluate another thought utilizing an altcoin; altcoins can be viewed as an innovative work proving ground for potential Bitcoin highlights. The pragmatic consequence is that there is some strain between supporters of Bitcoin and those of altcoins, yet also a feeling of a joint effort.

As of now, Bitcoin's hash power dwarfs that of the other altcoin. Indeed,Bitcoin has powerful miners and mining pools that management a lot of mining power than those deployed for entire altcoins. Such a laborer or entity might easily perform an attack against a tiny low altcoin (if it uses an equivalent SHA-256 mining puzzle as Bitcoin), inflicting forks and general disturbance, which are often adequate to kill the altcoin. we tend to decision this development altcoin infanticide.

Why would anyone do this, given that they must use their valuable mining power to do so and won't gain a significant monetary reward? Take the case of the 2012 attack on a small altcoin called CoiledCoin: the operator of the Bitcoin mining pool Eligius decided that CoiledCoin was a scam and an affront to the cryptocurrency ecosystem. So Eligius pointed its mining resources at CoiledCoin, mining blocks that reversed days' worth of CoiledCoin transaction history as well as mining a long chain with empty blocks, effectively causing a denial-of-service attack, which prevented

CoiledCoin users from making any transactions. After a fairly short siege, users abandoned CoiledCoin, and it no longer exists. In this example and other altcoin infanticide attacks, the attacker is motivated by something other than direct profit.

# Crytocurrency Mining

### Mining Power

In the event that two altcoins utilize a similar mining riddle, we can straightforwardly analyze them by how much mining force all the altcoin's diggers have. This is frequently just called the "hash rate" because of the noticeable quality of hash-based riddles. For model, Zetacoin is an altcoin that utilizations SHA-256 mining perplexes, similarly as Bitcoin does, and it has a system hash rate of around 5 terahashes/second ($5 \times 10\ 12$ hashes/second) as of December 2015. This number is around a hundred-thousandth of Bitcoin's mining power. It's trickier to consider the mining power between coins that usage particular mining befuddles, in light of the fact that the conundrums may put aside different proportions of exertion to enroll. Also, mining equipment concentrated for one of the coins won't really be used for mining (counting assaulting) the other coin. Notwithstanding for an altcoin utilizing a totally extraordinary mining riddle, we can at present take in something from the relative change in mining control after some time. Development in mining force demonstrates either that more members have joined or on the other hand that they have moved up to all the more dominant mining hardware. Loss of mining power, as a rule, implies a few diggers have relinquished the altcoin and is ordinarily an inauspicious sign.

## Merge Mining

By default—say, if an altcoin forks the Bitcoin source code but makes no other changes—mining on the altcoin is exclusive. That is, you can try to solve the mining puzzle solution to find a valid block for the altcoin or for Bitcoin, but you can't try to solve both puzzles at once. Of course, you can divide your mining resources to dedicate some to mining on the altcoin and some to mining on Bitcoin. You can even divide among multiple different altcoins and adjust your allocations over time, but there's no way to get your mining power to do double duty.

With merge mining, network effects can make it difficult for an altcoin to bootstrap. If you wanted to launch an altcoin and convince today's Bitcoin miners to participate in your network, they would have to stop mining Bitcoin (with at least some of their resources), which would mean an immediate loss of Bitcoin mining rewards. This means your altcoin is likely to remain small in terms of hashing power and more vulnerable to infanticide-style attacks by Bitcoin miners.

Would we be able to structure an altcoin with the goal that it's conceivable to mine squares both on the altcoin and on Bitcoin in the meantime? To do that, we have to make obstructs that incorporate exchanges from both Bitcoin and the altcoin, making them valid in both block chains. It's easy to design the altcoin so that it allows Bitcoin transactions in its blocks because we can write the rules of the altcoin however we want. The reverse is harder. Where can we put altcoin transactions in Bitcoin blocks?

There's a trick, though: even if we can't put the contents of the altcoin'

transactions into Bitcoin blocks, we can put a summary of the altcoin

transactions into Bitcoin blocks in the form of a hash pointer to the altcoin

block. Finding a way to put a single hash pointer into each Bitcoin block is

easy. Specifically, recall that each Bitcoin block has a special transaction—

the coinbase transaction—that the miner uses to create new coins as a block

reward. The scriptSig field of this transaction has no significance and can, therefore, be used to store arbitrary data (there's no need to sign the

Coinbase transaction, since it's not spending any previous transaction

outputs). So in a merge-mined altcoin, the mining task is to compute Bitcoin blocks whose Coinbase scriptSig contains a hash pointer to an altcoin block. This block can now do double duty: to Bitcoin clients, it looks just like any other Bitcoin block, with a hash in the coinbase transaction that can be ignored. Altcoin clients know how to interpret the block by ignoring them Bitcoin transactions and looking at the altcoin transactions committed to by the hash in the coinbase transaction. Although this doesn't require any changes to Bitcoin, it does require the altcoin to specifically understand Bitcoin and accept merge-mined blocks.

If our altcoin is merge mined, we hope that many Bitcoin miners will mine it, because doing so doesn't require any additional hash power. It requires a modicum of additional computational resources for processing blocks and transactions, and miners need to know and care enough about our altcoin to bother to mine it. Suppose that 25 percent of Bitcoin miners by hash power is mining our altcoin. Then on average, 25 percent of Bitcoin blocks contain pointers to altcoin blocks. It seems, then, that in our altcoin a new block would be mined on average every 40 minutes. Worse, while the altcoin is still being bootstrapped and the fraction of Bitcoin miners mining it is tiny, the time between blocks will be hours or days, which is unacceptable.

Can we ensure that blocks of a merge-mined altcoin are created at a steady rate, as high or low as we want, irrespective of the fraction of Bitcoin miners mining it? The answer is yes. The trick is that even though the mining task for the altcoin is the same as that for Bitcoin, the mining target need not be. The altcoin network computes the target and difficulty for its blocks independently of the Bitcoin network. Just as Bitcoin adjusts its mining target so that blocks are found every 10 minutes on average, the altcoin would adjust its own target, so that blocks in the altcoin are found every 10 minutes (or any other fixed interval)

Conversely, every valid altcoin block results from an attempt at mining a Bitcoin block, but only 30 percent of them actually meet Bitcoin's difficulty target. For the other 70 percent of altcoin blocks, the altcoin network needs to be able to verify the mining puzzle solution. The simple way to do this is to broadcast the Bitcoin near-block in addition to the altcoin block. But a cleverer way is to broadcast just the header of the Bitcoin near-block and the Merkle proof of inclusion of the Coinbase transaction in the Bitcoin block.

It's additionally conceivable (albeit infrequently observed) for the altcoin to have a more troublesome riddle than Bitcoin has. This is uncommon, on the grounds that generally altcoins need to have squares discovered more frequently than once per 10 minutes, however on the off chance that for some reason you needed a slower rate, it is anything but difficult to accomplish. In this case, you would see some Bitcoin hinders that the digger trusted would likewise become altcoin squares, yet they would be dismissed on the altcoin arrange, since they neglected to meet the harder trouble target.

### Union Mining and Security

Union mining is a big gift. It makes bootstrapping simpler, as we've talked about, and the subsequent lift to your altcoin's all out hash control builds its versatility to assault. A foe who is hoping to purchase registering capacity to pulverize your altcoin should make a tremendous direct front speculation. In any case, one could contend this is a misguided sensation that all is well and good, in light of the fact that such a foe would apparently recover the expense of his speculation by mining Bitcoin and the minor expense to assault your altcoin is trifling. This is simpler to acknowledge whether we consider a foe who is as of now an enormous Bitcoin excavator. To be sure, CoiledCoin, the altcoin that endured child murder (portrayed before in this area), was consolidation mined. The Eligius mining pool and its members did not have to stop Bitcoin mining to assault CoiledCoin. Truth be told, the pool members were not by any means mindful that their processing assets were being utilized in the assault! By mulling over a sound digger choosing whether or not to consolidate mine, we can find more issues with the security of union mining. Review that, generally, mining bodes well if the normal reward approaches or surpasses the normal expenses. For Bitcoin mining, the expense is essentially that of hash calculation. Be that as it may, for somebody who's as of now a Bitcoin digger choosing whether to union mine an altcoin, there is no extra expense from hashing. Rather, the extra expenses emerge from two factors: the the calculation, data transfer capacity, and capacity expected to approve the altcoin exchanges and the need to stay up with the latest and maybe make educated choices if the altcoin is experiencing hard or delicate forks.

This thinking yields two bits of knowledge. In the first place, combine mining has solid economies of scale, since all excavators acquire generally similar expenses

despite their hash control. This is as a glaring difference to Bitcoin, where cost is corresponding to hash control, to a first estimation. So for a low-value altcoin, a little solo excavator will think that its unrewarding to union mine it, since the expense surpasses the small reward they will make because of they're low hash control. Remember that starting in 2015, the potential income from mining altcoins remains a little division of Bitcoin mining income. This contention predicts that contrasted with Bitcoin, consolidate mined altcoins will have a more noteworthy centralization or grouping of mining power.

A related expectation is that most diggers will re-appropriate their exchange approvals. The littler the altcoin, the more prominent the motivating force to redistribute will be. The regular method to do this is to join a Bitcoin mining

pool. That is on the grounds that pools normally remove those calculations from excavators' hands. The pool administrator gathers a Bitcoin hinder that fuses squares

from (at least zero) altcoins, in the wake of approving the exchanges in the Bitcoin obstruct just as any altcoin squares. The digger just attempts to understand for the nonce. These expectations are borne out practically speaking. For instance, GHash.IO, at one time the biggest Bitcoin mining pool permits union mining of Namecoin, IXCoin, and DevCoin. So those monetary forms turned into the most well, known union mined altcoins.

The second understanding from the monetary thinking is maybe much more stressing for security than the grouping of mining power. Whenever diggers' essential expense is confirmation of work, by configuration, there is no chance to get for excavators to game the framework. There is no alternate way to mining, given the security of hash capacities and moreover different excavators effectively can and will confirm the verification of work. The two suspicions bomb when the expense is that of exchange approval. An excavator could expect that exchanges they found out about are legitimate and plan to pull off not checking them. In addition, for other excavators to approve a square and its exchanges are the same amount of work as it was for the digger who discovered it. Therefore, we ought to anticipate that in any event for little union excavators, there's an impetus to hold back on approval. The

presence of inappropriately approving diggers makes assaults simpler, on the grounds that a malevolent excavator can make a square that will make the remainder of the diggers differ on what the longest substantial branch is. To abridge, consolidate mining tackles one security issue yet makes numerous others, to some degree in light of the fact that the financial aspects of union mining vary in significant ways from the financial aspects of select mining. By and large, it's far from clear that consolidation mining is a smart thought for another altcoin concerned about mining assaults

## Ethereum and Smart Contracts

We have seen a few different ways to utilize Bitcoin's scripting language to help fascinating applications, for example, an escrowed installment exchange. Namecoin was the main model, yet numerous others have proposed digital forms of money much like Bitcoin however supporting betting, stock issuance, forecast markets, thus

onwards. Imagine a scenario in which, rather than expecting to dispatch another framework to help each application, we manufactured a digital currency that could bolster any application we might devise later on? This is the thing that Turing fulfillment is about: a Turing-complete programming language gives you a chance to indicate any usefulness that is conceivable to program into a Turing machine, a dynamic model of a PC that is accepted to be equipped for processing any capacity that can be processed by any stretch of the imagination. As a result, each Turing-complete programming language—including natural ones, for example, Java, Python, and Lisp—is indistinguishable in the arrangement of calculations that it permits to be communicated. In a certain hypothetical sense, Turing fulfillment is as well as can be expected trust in a programming language as far as expressive power, disregarding down to earth matters, for example, effortlessness and execution.

Somewhat, the circumstance today harkens back to the beginning of PCs themselves during the 1940s: progressively muddled machines were being worked for different explicit applications during World War II, (for example, animal driving keys utilized by mechanical figure machines or deciding terminating directions for maritime mounted guns), spurring specialists to construct the first, re-programmable broadly useful PCs that could be utilized for any possible applications.

# Bitcoin as a Global Reserve Currency

**Bitcoin May Become A Global Reserve Instrument**

Bitcoin in its present state isn't tied in with making worldwide micropayments at almost no charge. Bitcoin is about a safe haven for financial and information resources while at the same time introducing another type of developing an economy, one where the constituents are definitely not bound by legal enactment and simple types of trade. The bitcoin advanced the economy may turn into a worldwide save instrument because of elements which are made conceivable by sound monetary standards and the specialized perfection brought by blockchain systems and their guarantees for advancement. In this post, I'd like to take a brief take a gander at three of those elements. Bitcoin can possibly lessen business spins through inelastic supply work. The supply issuance of new money units is administered by a numerical calculation instead of a national bank money related approach. No adjustment popular has an impact on the rate of this issuance, and in this way, makes the supply capacity of bitcoin inelastic. Vacillations popular have no impact on the supply timetable of bitcoin, The ability to pay is spoken to by the gliding section in national cash. The mining trouble calculation is equipped for self-acclimating to changes in the rivalry among mining pools. Strikingly, this speaks to one of only a handful couple of structures of self-administration the bitcoin convention has.

The Austrian school of money related thought holds that the bust of a business cycle is unpreventable, what should be kept up a key separation from rather is a phony and a portion of the time misleading impact in the market, which does no value for addressing the soundness of the economy. One of the main considerations of encouraging a blast is credit development, an open door for credit extensions in bitcoin are constrained because of the trouble of fragmentary save practices and quantitative facilitating (if a wonder such as this can truly in bitcoin is

another contention).

Bitcoin can possibly make financial players less reliant upon others in the equivalent or nearby markets. The openness prerequisites of bitcoin are extraordinarily low. Frameworks which are made open advantage hugely from the system impact and bitcoin just requires a cell phone with a web network. On the off chance that clients want to lead exchanges over the bitcoin connect with no compelling reason to gain endorsement, it guarantees to possibly make every client less subject to each other member in the framework. At the point when people require no outer consent, they are enabled. For whatever length of time that one gathering does not control the whole system, clients remain generally free and in control of their own monetary occupation. Encryption has at no other time empowered monetary resources (information resources as well) to be put away so modestly with such a high level of security.

Diminish Diamandis depicts demonetization in his 'exponential structure' as one of the key stages. With respect to bitcoin, this depicts the demonetization of numerous parts of our current money related framework (banking charges, ATM expenses, settlement expenses, bank foundation, banking representative compensations). Bitcoin is demonetization of our current budgetary framework since it can relieve and kill this outsider prerequisites. The innovation of encryption makes, for the absolute first time, assurance of our monetary resources both exceptionally secure and extremely cheap. In truth, when bitcoin is utilized as it is intended to be utilized (as a connection among you and your cash with no prerequisite of trust), the possibility of a fruitful hack is close to 0. Encryption of the blockchain likewise gives the possibility to verify and transmit data resources (as well as money related), cheaply with a high level of security and straightforwardness. Bitcoin may keep on being progressively utilized as a worldwide hold instrument for both financial and information resources since it possibly mitigate business goes through an inelastic supply work makes clients less reliant upon adjoining members in the economy, and permits a high level of security effortlessly because of advances in cryptography.

**Bitcoin Will End the Nation State**

Satoshi Nakamoto set in movement the disentangling of the country state and the finish of focal banking ... two firmly related organizations that have coordinated history since history has been recorded. When we come to comprehend the monetary and innovative ramifications of bitcoin, we land at a to some degree alarming yet certain end: that bitcoin will end the country state.

**Bitcoin as an Economy Independent of the Nation-State**

Numerous onlookers of bitcoin contend that its worth should be pegged to a stable, ordinary cash so as to survey its worth. They guarantee that bitcoin is as well unpredictable to be paid attention to, and in this way, fills in as just a novel budgetary and mechanical advancement for moving cash. What these spectators' neglect to acknowledge is that bitcoin shouldn't be pegged to a national cash anything else than the sun requires the gravitational draw of the earth. The sun has no worry for the the gravitational draw of the Earth similarly as bitcoin has no worry for the improvements inside national economies. The theory is the main reason pundits will contend that Bitcoin should be pegged to a national unit of record, and for those on-screen characters, bitcoin cares not.

Numerous eyewitnesses of bitcoin additionally contend that for selection, bitcoin needs trade organizations and ATMs so as to develop its client base and in this way, its advertise capitalization. Over these organizations, the traditional mastermind will likewise contend that legitimate guideline should be implemented on these activities for the 'great of the financial specialist'. We surely don't need another scene of Mt.Gox do we Although trade organizations and ATMs absolutely serve to hurry the selection procedure, they are not required for the development of the bitcoin economy. The mining procedure fills in as the issuance expert. The diggers are the workers of the bitcoin the system, and subsequently the genuine residents in the advanced economy.

## Bitcoin is an [Nationally] Untaxable Money Supply

Give us a chance to start with a straightforward reason: you can't demand assesses on an encoded cash supply through a legal specialist. Bitcoin is unapproachable by the country state and can be utilized possibly secretly. In his Code 2.0 pronouncement, Lawrence Lessig portrayed the law as a variety of variables, guideline being only one among many. Different variables incorporate the free market, social standards, and engineering. In the bitcoin economy engineering is source-code. Really, bitcoin is code as law and the blockchain speaks to a kind of constitution for the computerized economy.

No measure of campaigning, congressional hearings, orbit licenses will make a

the quantifiable effect over the long haul. Since bitcoin is unapproachable by the country express, the soul of these ordinary bodies or governments will wilt and kick the bucket. Progressively, government officials will battle to crush the income from their residents in request to pay for the consistently swelling costs and projects it has considered. Whenever the the backbone of the country express, the assessment incomes, have run dry, that is the point at which we can certainly, announce that the incredible domains of countries are dead. The domains whose watch managed the progression and annihilation of society to limits already inconceivable, will be no more.

**Bitcoin Transitions the Nature of Violence**

The most overwhelming money today is held set up on the grounds that the specialist which issues it has the best capacity to force and protect from brutality. The United States Federal Reserve Note is the worldwide save money, not as a result of the country's unwavering confidence in opportunity, or the sound money related approaches of its pioneers. The USD is the world money in light of the fact that, as we have found in times past, when somebody takes steps to isolate themselves from their reliance of it, along these lines settling its situation as the ruler, the expert subverts its own laws and looks to devastate those who might endeavor to incapacitate its strength?

Bitcoin, then again, rises above physicality and can't be crushed by any country state. In the digital space, the monetary profits for viciousness change to the individuals who are equipped for executing cyberwarfare and robberies through the vehicle of computerized innovation itself, The cyber domain is and will keep on being a shelter for those with the specialized insight to direction a machine to do what they need it to, rather then the first guidelines it was given. Since bitcoin advances the burglary of cash and the issuance of cash to the computerized domain, the nature of brutality also is put inside a setting which must be followed up on by members who stay on the internet. What sorts of brutality could be forced through money related modes of a computerized domain?

One such model we have seen is the ascent of ransomware. Ransomware is a kind of an infection which secures significant documents and just opens them after a specific sum of bitcoin have been sent to a location. This sort of cybercrime is as of now causing enormous interruptions among partnerships and will keep on having significant suggestions for the intercession of wrongdoing and the advanced medium. Another demonstration of brutality could be viewed as the collectivization of information on the development, possessions, and relationship of budgetary data in an advanced economy for example, bitcoin. An immense motivation presents itself for information mining the blockchain and breaking down the different connections and examples of spending. Much like the web of today, the bitcoin organize at first introduces itself as a bastion of freedom and secrecy yet is in truth bound to turn into the most surveillance type of cash ever to exist.

All that you've come to think about government benefits, social welfare projects, and nationality as a philosophy, will be devastated by the ramifications of bitcoin. We have a developing computerized economy, which for the absolute first time, can work totally free of physical or focal entertainers. We have a cash supply which depends on the exploration of science and hence has its very use supported by a human appropriate to the right to speak freely, yet more significantly, we now

have a cash supply which is made in fact unfeasible to impose with our current

systems because of encryption innovation. We have a system of money related data which changes the idea of savagery, that of cybercrime, to the advanced domain.

These variables joined will guarantee that the country state as it exists today will be

unalterably upset in a societal move inconspicuous since the ousting of religious foundations during the fifteenth and sixteenth for hundreds of years. This time, the real contrast is that it will happen considerably more rapidly and have substantially more inescapable impacts than nearly anybody is foreseeing End.A few people are amped up for Bitcoin on account of the fundamental innovation. Others are amped up for its business potential outcomes, but others about its social and political ramifications. Sensible individuals can differ about the last two, yet we trust this book has persuaded you that innovatively, Bitcoin is profound, novel, intriguing, and dependent on sound standards. Past Bitcoin is a captivating universe of option

cryptographic money plans that we're simply beginning to investigate, some of which might one day easily compare to Bitcoin itself. We got into Bitcoin in light of the fact that we trust in the intensity of its innovation, also, we believe it's profoundly associated with the remainder of software engineering. While we've featured how apparently astonishing new innovation can battle to uproot built up foundations, we accept that over the long haul individuals will keep on finding new economically and socially valuable activities with digital money innovation. Regardless of whether your advantage is fundamentally business, you'd do well to ace the fundamental innovation—getting itspower and confinements will enable you to more readily climate the market's publicity cycles.

What would be an ideal next step? A standout amongst the best things about decentralization is that it's an incredible stage for experimentation and learning. Anybody can download and dissect Bitcoin's square chain, or assemble their very own applications over it; we trust you'll exploit these opportunities.

## Digital Currency Wallet

Digital money wallets are programming applications that store your open and private keys and interface with different blockchains and give functionalities to check the parity, send cash, and lead different activities. At the point when a wallet client sends Bitcoins or some other sort of advanced money to you, they are essentially closing down responsibility for coins to the sender's wallet address. To have the option to understand the assets, the private key put away in your wallet programming must match the open location the cash is connected to. On the off chance that open and private keys of the sender and collector coordinate, the equalization in your wallet programming will increment, and thusly the sender's record parity will diminish. There is no real trade of physical coins. The exchange is inferred only by an exchange record on the blockchain and an adjustment in parity in your cryptographic money wallet.

Give us now a chance to comprehend this procedure with a model. Give Mark a chance to be a client who has a Bitcoin wallet and is currently prepared to get reserves.

• Once Mark agrees to accept a Bitcoin account, his wallet application will ran Faintly create a private key together with its relating Bitcoin address.

• His Bitcoin address is only a number that relates to a key that he can use to control access to the assets. There is no relationship between that address and a record.

• Until the minute when this location is taking an interest in a Bitcoin transaction as a sender or a (beneficiary) of significant worth posted on the Bitcoin record (the

blockchain), it is basically part of the huge number of conceivable addresses that are substantial in a Bitcoin.

• Once the location has been related with an exchange, it turns out to be a piece of the distinguished locations in the system and Mark can check his equalization on the open record.

Suppose Mark possesses a coffeehouse and a client, state, Harry, decides to pay for supper utilizing Bitcoins. Imprint has shown his location or the QR code of his Bitcoin address at the highest point of the menu board in his shop for his customers to have the option to pay with their Bitcoins. This is the open key of this wallet which is utilized for getting the assets. How about we believe the expense for supper to be

0.10 Bitcoin, otherwise called 100 millibits. To move the Bitcoins to Mark's account, if Harry is utilizing the blockchain portable wallet on an Android telephone, he would see a screen mentioning two data sources:

1. Beneficiary: The goal Bitcoin address for the exchange

2. Worth: The measure of Bitcoin to send

**Types of Wallets**

There are five unique sorts of wallets accessible for advanced money that provide various approaches to store and access your coins safely. Wallets can be classified into three particular classifications—programming, equipment, and paper.

**Bitcoin exchange—true situation**

1. Work area wallets are intended for PCs and Mac, which must be downloaded and introduced on the PC. Once introduced, they are just accessible from a similar PC in which they are introduced. Work area wallets are increasingly secure; be that as it may, if your PC is hacked or tainted by an infection at that point there is the likelihood of you losing every one of your assets.

2. Online wallets are cloud-based programming available from any PC from any area. They are exceptionally simple to get to, however online wallets store your private keys in a brought together online capacity and are overseen by a third party, which makes them helpless against hacking assaults and robbery.

3. Versatile wallets are programming applications accessible on your preferred portable application store for download and establishment on your cell phones. These are the most helpful of the considerable number of wallets that can be utilized from anyplace counting retail locations. Versatile wallets are more straightforward than work area wallets due to asset restrictions on the versatile, yet they give the majority of the essential highlights required for the greater part of the exchanges.

4. Equipment wallets store a client's private key in an equipment gadget, for example, USB. Hardware wallets give choices to make online exchanges in a profoundly verified design by putting away the client's private keys in a disconnected storage. Equipment wallets are good to be utilized over various conventions also, bolster numerous cryptographic forms of money. Clients interface the wallet to their

web empowered PC by means of the USB, enter their PIN or secret key to login to the wallet, and begin making exchanges. Equipment wallets come with a more expensive rate point, however they are the best wallet for genuine cryptocurrency possessions where spending a little total toward verifying the private keys is amazingly basic to shield the estimation of the advantages you claim on the blockchain.


5. Paper wallets are a totally separated non-electronic method for putting away the private keys. They are essentially a physical duplicate of your open and private keys on paper. It is an old school customary methodology of keeping up your mystery yourself. Moving Bitcoin or some other kind of cryptocurrency to your paper wallet is moderately clear and includes transfer of coins from an electronic wallet to the open location showed on the printout of your paper wallet. To pull back or send coins to another wallet, you should move assets from the paper wallet to a product wallet. This procedure is alluded to as clearing which should be possible either physically entering your private keys or examining a QR code that ordinarily prints on

the paper wallet.


## Wallet Security


As we discussed in the past section, wallets are secure to fluctuating degrees and subject to the sort of wallet and the item provider. Online wallets are inherently less secure on account of the joined accumulating of the private keys, along these lines uncovering clients to the vulnerabilities in the electronic stage which in uncommon cases can be abused by programmers to take your benefits on a blockchain. Then again, equipment wallets are exceedingly secure as they store client's private keys disconnected however accompany a sticker price and trouble in getting to your keys for making the transactions. Albeit online wallets are inclined to cyberattacks, it is exceptionally fitting to play it safe when utilizing any sort of wallet.


Continuously recollect, losing your private keys is identical to losing your cash. Whichever wallet you use, you should play it safe and be exceptionally cautious!

In the event that your wallet gets hacked or you send cash to an inaccurate location or to a con artist, there is positively no real way to recuperate lost money or turn around the transaction. We should now take a gander at certain precautionary measures that will keep you from extraordinary misfortune.

**1. Reinforcing the Keys**—Backing up your digital currency wallet can save you from a lot of trouble but it is on the cost of a severe danger which is that your phone or the laptop you have saved your stuff on might get lost and you might lose all your coins and while this method has a benefits on one side but severe disadvantages on the other.

**2. Cold Storage**—Cold stockpiling is accomplished when digital currency private keys are made and put away in a protected disconnected condition. Cold stockpiling is significant for anybody with high-esteem crypto possessions. Online PCs are helpless

to programmers and ought not be utilized to store a lot of Bitcoins.

**3. Equipment Wallet**—These are the physical gadgets made to keep your digital money safe. When you demand an installment, the equipment wallet's Programming interface makes and signs the exchange and gives an open key which is coordinated to the system by the API.    This guarantees the marking keys never leave the equipment wallet. Equipment wallets accompany support for propelled highlights, for example, multi-signature exchanges.

**4. Multi-Signature**—Wallets are propelled security setup accessible with the vast majority of the digital currency stages and bolstered by a large portion of the prominent wallets. It includes numerous partners to be associated with an exchange.

# ICO Regulatory and Reporting Framework

There are incredible forecasts on the capability of blockchain-based answers for "change" everything from budgetary markets to the very way that we through and through perceive human character for billions of individuals around the world. Beginning arrangements on blockchain were increasingly revolved around the money related industry, yet the pattern has moved presently to address a wide cluster of divisions, and most of them have a social effect. In the present world, innovation is engaging society to explore with new arrangements and plans of action. Blockchain is a sort of innovation that has the ability to manage noteworthy wasteful aspects and change activities in the social segment and to improve our way of life.

Blockchain's inborn attributes of permanence, decentralizetion, and straightforwardness help construct trust over various frameworks. In this chapter, we will show blockchain's ability to make adaptable social sway and to recognize the components that should be accounted for to alleviate challenges in its application.

How about we consider a couple of genuine occasions; blockchain applications could provide the methods for building up personalities for people without ID cards, presenting money and banking administrations for the underprovisioned class of

populaces and helping help appropriations to outcasts with improved transparency and productivity. Governments over the globe are taking estimations to put land library data onto blockchains to improve straightforwardness and dodge outsider debasement and control. Blockchain's endless potential applications for social effect run from expanding access to funding to following wellbeing and training information over different ages, to improving voter records and casting a ballot frameworks.

The social impacts of blockchain can be incredible and enduring, while developers take on structure these kinds of arrangements. Blockchain has the potential to significantly effective from the structure, application, and approach to the improvement. With this sort of potential, the execution of blockchain advances has long haul suggestions for society and people.

This section diagrams why announcing is especially essential with blockchain furthermore, offers a structure to direct policymakers and social effect associations

to settle on fitting structure choices to empower revealing appropriate from the development of the arrangement. As web based life, digital forms of money, and calculations have appeared, innovation isn't impartial. Qualities are implanted in the code. It is imperative to comprehend the way in which the issue is characterized and by whom, who is building the arrangement, the technique where it gets customized

furthermore, executed, who approaches, and what standards are made have consequences in purposeful and inadvertent ways. In the applications and usage of blockchain, it is fundamental to understand that evidently innocuous structure choices have resounding good consequences on people's lives. It is fundamental to ensure that genuine courses of action are made in the structure for the required level of uncovering.

**Plan Considerations for Reporting**

Once blockchain turns out as proper innovation, it is essential to analyze the accompanying zones important to guarantee there is sufficient detailing coverage in the framework. At each stage, directing inquiries distinguish the impacts of the plan decisions on the end clients and networks. Straightforward Unchanging nature Trust One of a kind mixes of conduct

**1. Administration**—How is administration made and kept up?

**2. Personality**—How is character characterized and set up?

**3. Confirmation and Authentication**—How are information sources checked and transactions validated?

**4. Access Control**—How is access characterized, in truth, and executed?

**5. Information Ownership**—How is the responsibility for characterized, in truth, and executed?

**6. Security**—The way where security is set up and guaranteed.

**Administration**

Administration alludes to the foundation and upkeep of the principles that administer the whole blockchain framework. A principal normal for blockchain innovation is having an inflexible arrangement of principles by which all exchanges inside the framework are administered. In the social division, it is basic to guarantee that a sound human administration structure is driving the innovation. Administration incorporates questions, for example, who sets up the principles, who keeps up the framework, how the principles are executed, and how a blockchain framework would be finished off. The built up administration structure ought to likewise be in charge of guaranteeing adherence to the core values and plan theory of the venture.

Following are the key plan contemplations for providing details regarding Governance:

• Determining who the partners are, their jobs, and how their jobs are set up.

• Establishing the procedures, guidelines, and guidelines of administration (both technical and something else).

• Creating pathways for these principles and jobs to change after some time.

• Having an arrangement for finishing off or proceeding with the framework if key partners leave.

## Personality

Huge moral contemplations encompass what establishes "character" and to whom personality is conceded in a given blockchain, and the way wherein personality data is utilized, gotten to, and ensured. Numerous bits of identifying data on the whole make a computerized character. Blockchains can be used to build up constrained, or value-based, advanced characters for getting to data or administrations. Versatile, primary advanced characters can likewise be built up utilizing blockchain frameworks. Convenient, central computerized characters are the personalities that are for all time connected to a special individual and henceforth can be utilized in an assortment of settings, moving with the person, to demonstrate personality or accreditations.

Following are the key plan contemplations for giving an account of Identity:

• Understand who is allowed personality in this specific circumstance.

• Understand the arrangement personality level.

– Note: a value-based personality can be considered as a restricted reason personality. It allows an individual single-use or constrained access to a specific service. Then again, a basic personality fills in as a completely functioning character that can be utilized for some reasons after some time.

• Determine the identifiers that will be utilized to establish this element.

• Prevent presentation of by and by recognizable data on a blockchain.

– This may require never putting by and by recognizable data legitimately on a blockchain.

**Check and Authentication**

Check of sources of info and afterward its verification is significant in an open record

framework. The way toward confirming data put onto a blockchain accompanies a ton of difficulties. The confirmation procedure for computerized resources like cryptographic forms of money or on the other hand computerized photos is firmly identified with the exchange verification process. It is done to decide whether the substance that started an exchange has any control over that benefit. At the point when a non-advanced resource, for example, an individual or an article, is connected

to a blockchain, difficulty increments in confirmation since it presents human association and, accordingly, different political, lawful, and moral obstructions.

For example, by what means would someone be able to's guarantee of land proprietorship be checked?

Following are the key structure contemplations for giving an account of Verification what's more, Authentication:

• Determining how and by whom check will be accomplished for the underlying passage, or "zero state," pursue on information info, and how exchanges between

clients are verified.

– This incorporates setting up both data verifying procedures and technical structures that avert invalid passages.

• Ensuring that all partners can confide in the built up procedure.

• Understand any financial, lawful, political, and social effect of agreement convention calculations.

## Access Control

Access definition, conceding, and execution are basic for any individual for utilizing

what's more, connecting with a blockchain framework. Additionally, the extent of access to individuals' close to home data on a blockchain may result in genuine implications for those people if that data is abused. Past the points of interest of getting to a blockchain to view or keep in touch with the record, get to likewise incorporates progressively elusive inquiries around advanced education and the compelling capacity to get to the framework.

Following are the key plan contemplations for providing details regarding Access Control:

• Who has consents to compose?

• Who has authorizations to peruse?

• The way wherein the authorizations are built up.

• The degree of access that clients are given.

## Information Ownership

There are some significant inquiries like the proprietor of the information, who activities authority over the information, where and the way in which the information is put away, and how modifications are made to wrong data. An interesting characteristic of blockchain is its capacity to enable clients to practice utilitarian power over information. It can possibly respond to inquiries on the proprietor of the information, practicing command over the information, where and the way in which the information is put away, and how erroneous data is balanced. For instance, the Sovrin Foundation is building a self-sovereign personality trust system that makes a powerful administration structure that enables individuals to apply constructive control over their own computerized character data.

Following are the key structure contemplations for writing about Data Ownership:

• Understanding who possesses information, both in name and practically speaking.

• Knowing and understanding the way in which partners will be capable to utilize the claimed information and subsequently advantage from it.

• Deciding if information will be put away remotely or in the blockchain.

– Considering information stockpiling choices that are decentralized.

• Creating a procedure for clients where they will probably banner and fix erroneous data.

**Security**

A disseminated foundation can have information dissipated on top of it. This, thus, lessens the vulnerabilities contrasted and information that is amassed and put away in one area. It isn't important for clients to recollect passwords. Truth be told, it is likewise a bit much for them to interface their own data, similar to messages or on the other hand contact numbers, to accumulations of put away data. Nonetheless, there are moral difficulties here also. Blockchain security utilizes encryption calculations what's more, the utilization of open/private key combines that resemble a freely known "address" furthermore, a private computerized key to basically open the post box at that address. Blockchain advancements have been progressively utilized for verifying private data like wellbeing records. At an individual level, this alludes to a client's comprehension of potential dangers just as private key administration. At the framework level, this alludes to potential vulnerabilities inside and at the outskirts of the framework. What might occur if there should be an occurrence of loss of computerized key that is utilized to control resources or therapeutic data?

Following are the key plan contemplations for providing details regarding Data Ownership:

• Determining who builds up security just as who is in charge of rupturing it.

• To guarantee that defenseless information is sufficiently ensured against current and future dangers.

• Deciding the way in which various snippets of data will be secured.

• Creating a framework for protected and compelling access to private keys.

# Blockchain Ecosystem

Any arrangement on blockchain is driven by a biological system contained of these factors: the client, network, existing foundation, and financials. In this manner, it is significant from a revealing point of view to direct a biological system assessment. This evaluation will help to understand and recognize the jobs that every one of these center parts plays in adding to the blockchain-based arrangement. The jobs of these segments are for the most part associated by means of a snare of complex collaborations. These jobs may fluctuate all through the venture course of events. Be that as it may, biological systems are not static, they are liquid and along these lines keep on evolving what's more, advance all through the whole life cycle of the venture. It is critical to comprehend regular changes to the environment as well as the way in which the usage and the plan of a blockchain arrangement may influence (hurry or goad) these procedures. The evaluation ought to likewise be occasionally returned to advise and assess key plan decisions. It ought to likewise be refreshed furthermore, reevaluated as the venture advances.

**Blockchain Potential**

Since the job of chronicle and putting away data and information is essential for the administration, they have the enduring obligation to have a framework that is based upon trust. Residents must believe that their data and information is secure with the legislature. Our residents' most fundamental data and information must be secure from hacks and ruptures from inside our fringes and outside our state furthermore, nation. The nature and innovation of blockchain appears to be extremely encouraging in a world where government must give a place of refuge to putting away and moving records. The circulated nature and trust confirmation procedure of blockchain is possibly of incredible use to our administration and must be optimized and actualized quickly. The sending of these center advances can lead to a progressively straightforward and proficient government and advantage society.

## Clients

At the beginning of the environment evaluation, the end clients of a blockchain instrument must be distinguished, and in this way the biological system must be comprehended from the end clients' point of view. Understanding this end-client viewpoint includes inside and out research and discussions. It additionally includes a comprehensive plan procedure to completely comprehend the personality of the end clients, their requirements, their vulnerabilities, and some other dangers they may confront. Every one of these necessities, vulnerabilities, and dangers in the present state just as their potential development in conceivable future contexts must be assessed.

## Client Assessment Questions

• Who are the clients?

– Important key traits of the clients. Advanced proficiency of clients. Setting education of clients.

– The explanation for these being the end clients of the ideal result.

• Needs/objectives of the clients.

– The way wherein these might change after some time.

• Vulnerabilities of the clients

– The way where these might change after some time.

• Risks to the clients.

– The way where these might change after some time.

## Network

Notwithstanding recognizing the end clients of the blockchain, their personality and

network additionally should be comprehended. This incorporates understanding the borders of the network, or networks. The elements inside and between them likewise should be comprehended. At the point when a network is thought of it as, is essential to focus on what elements and fundamental powers are having an effect on everything, as well as the jobs and connections of the majority of the network individuals irrespective of their being immediate blockchain end clients. Building up this sort of understanding requires collaboration from network individuals to distinguish, for model, who could give a decent or administration that is basic to the ideal result, who could give the personality important to get to that great or administration, and who in the network could validate the legitimacy of the character claims.

## Network Assessment Questions

• The pertinent limits of the network that incorporates physical, social, social, and monetary.

– Possibility of these limits clashing with each other.

• Relationships that are significant in the network.

– Nominal power holder in the network.

– Effective power holder in the network.

– The way where the appropriation of intensity is built up.

– Possibility of having minimized or helpless network individuals. The likelihood of having inside dangers to specific individuals from the network.

– Are these connections formalized or casual?


• Relationship of the network with outer entertainers.

– The different outer associations that have connections inside the network. The association with all network individuals or a specific subset.

– Possibility of any outer dangers to individuals from the network.


• Community-level needs/objectives.

– The change it may acquire what's to come.


• What are network level vulnerabilities?

– How may these adjustment later on?


• What are network level dangers?

– How may these adjustment later on? (Consider the development of technology, environmental change, changes in power.)


**Foundation**


It is essential to comprehend the framework that ties individuals from the community together for accomplishing another ideal result. Legitimate and administrative structures, open arrangements, casual standards or frameworks, and information and other resources could be a piece of this foundation. Utilizing these structures can be done to accomplish the ideal result. It might likewise make grating or obstructions during the usage of blockchain apparatuses. The possibility to make friction for these structures could happen at any phase of the task—from plan to advancement, to sending, to usage, to sustainment, to the potential end or change of blockchain instruments.


**Framework Assessment Questions**

• The way wherein the present framework achieves the result.

– Where in the process is improvement happening (efficient, cost sparing)? The likelihood of this improvement being reproduced by a totally new blockchain framework. If not, the way wherein the open door expenses of staying with the

old framework are adjusted.


• The strategies, lawful and administrative structures, casual frameworks, social furthermore, social frameworks, and different procedures that are set up which may influence the ideal result.

– The components of the framework that could be utilized in the blockchain arrangement.

– Factors or elements that may disturb or anticipate the execution of the arrangement.


• Current existing information.

– Ownership of the information.

– Accuracy of the information. Is there an all inclusive or sufficient acknowledgment of its precision?

– Preciseness of the information.

– Comprehensively of the information.

– The way where it is put away.


**Financials**


The usage of a blockchain apparatus is driven by budgetary motivating forces that impact each phase of the venture life cycle. In this way, it is imperative to understand the way where a blockchain would be financed, and who might advantage monetarily from its usage. Understanding who might be hurt monetarily from its usage and how budgetary obstacles may modify key plan decisions are additionally significant.


**Money related Assessment Questions**

- Financial motivating forces of the substance fabricating a blockchain.

- The way wherein the blockchain would be financed at each phase in the process.

- Financially who might profit by the usage of a blockchain furthermore, how?

- Financial impetuses that are required for keeping the present framework set up.

- Who might be hurt monetarily from the usage of another blockchain?

- Sustainability of the financing model for the blockchain.

- Are there money related obstacles that would drive plan choices?

- Would the subsequent plan choices increment or decline client utility?

- Would the subsequent plan choices increment or abatement client chance?

## Announcing

As united exercises are continually pushed to realize a rule structure around electronic financial structures when all is said in done, it is essential that business visionaries who are in this space be proactive and earth shattering and complete a reporting structure for any passage that a client faces in a cryptographic cash adventure. Generally detailing structures are incorporated into the first plans of stages and are more than regularly refilled or redistributed to outsider programming. It is increasingly judicious to play it safe on account of the very administrative nature of the security business to make actualizing a announcing system a high need. One of the numerous advantages of taking the approach of architecting the entryway around an administration system is that a revealing structure is instinctively plan. Owing to the dependence on a administration system that fuses member the executives holding fast to jobs, exercises, occasions qualifications, a characteristic revealing structure can be built. In light of the administration system a general parameterized detailing stage turns into a characteristic fit. As members are on boarded inside the system through an enrollment process an interesting scrambled ID is doled out to every individual or substance that wants to turn into an individual from the system. General data from that participant is gathered during this procedure alongside supporting documents to fulfill the KYC guidelines. All data experiences a verification procedure to affirm all data tolerating all candidates who pass the approval process and dismissing others. The KYC procedure is essential, in spite of the fact that it might seem to disregard the security and obscurity standards of crypto currencies. Isolating the engineering plan of the commercial center that characterizes the setting and exchange nature of the money from the hidden installments framework that encourages decentralized exchanges parts permits the harmony of the crypto endeavor to exist. Cryptographic money without a characterized commercial center dependent on chronicled investigation would be a game played among a specialty gathering of programming and innovation lovers. Achieving a minimum amount without a commercial center would be almost outlandish.

The commercial center is the worth added surface that carries pertinence to computerized currency. A trade off is come to keep the business people, who are bold enough to advocate development in computerized money, from enduring the danger of genuine lawful repercussions and having a feasible business. As illustrated, the administration system has a characteristic revealing structure as members are recorded utilizing a private profoundly verified system, a VPN.

The information model developed will incorporate one of a kind ID and area subtleties of people. Extra data important to the announcing procedure, such as beginning enlistment date, process date, and member date, should be recorded.

Executing this idea at an insignificant, utilizing these three kinds of dates reports, actual dates that members enrolled will give a component to report on how productive the commercial center is. The time contrast between an beginning enlistment and when the enrollment was formally recognized and started to wind up handled will give a sign of the proficiency of the organization and enlistment procedure of the commercial center. The time difference between the underlying enrollment date and the part date short the slack from the procedure date would give a sign about the effectiveness of the individual giving the confirmation documentation expected to fulfill registration prerequisites. These caption parameters give an understanding into managing proficiency to the proprietors of the gateway. On the off chance that the check procedure is taking longer than normal, they additionally give a notice to proprietors that people might give false data to get checked reports set up.

It is best for proprietors to have however much understanding as could reasonably be expected since they are the one confronting a legitimate hazard, as individuals come on the web and their record moves toward becoming dynamic and ready to hold cash. The administration system including occasions and activities will record part account movement and look after current position possessions. These subtleties start to shape some institutionalized reports that must be organized inside any money related record the board which are personal account rundown. Prior to spreading out the individual record rundown, we should investigate the general structure of the revealing system. The entry will permit revealing encounters dependent on the login jobs. In the event that the individual is a site executive they would have diverse announcing privileges than that of an individual client. An individual client may likewise have distinctive revealing highlights. To fulfill the base prerequisites for consistence, it is adequate to concentrate on administrating obligation of revealing jobs, individuals allotted to jobs, decides on movement levels that go over principle limits. Notwithstanding site chairmen giving administrative answering to administering specialists, offices to singular individuals is a prerequisite too.

Having the hidden framework to make records and labeled information elements from a characterized information model makes parameterized announcing conceivable. As a best work on, structuring the revealing establishment executing the Application Programming Interface is most basic to make a component rich client revealing knowledge. To give a base detailing set to fulfill regulators utilizing the characteristic summed up system begin by ordering out jobs. Every job classification will have an interesting ID, which could be a framework numeric ID. Ensure the model contains an alpha identifier up to a specific indicated length and contains a portrayal component that gives further lucidity

## The Economy of Bermuda

During the seventeenth century, the economy of Bermuda was whaling, shipbuilding, developing tobacco, and the beginning of the salt-raking exchange with the Turks and Caicos Islands. Between the 1600s and the 1800s, the economy was energized by servitude which wasn't canceled in Bermuda until 1834. The 1700s additionally observed Bermuda become a privateering economy because of threats among England and Europe. During the 1800s, sending out vegetables, particularly Bermuda onions, in the spring toward the eastern US turned into the pillar of the economy together with the developing and sending of Bermuda Easter lilies (Lilium longiflorum) and bulbs. With mellow temperatures, staggering excellence, and under 700 miles from the US, in the late 1800s and mid 1900s, Bermuda developed as a prominent vacation goal among well off Americans. Creator and humorist Mark

Twain broadly expressed, "You can go to paradise on the off chance that you need to. I'd preferably remain in Bermuda." Tourism was the backbone of Bermuda's economy until the 1980s when it was gradually supplanted by global business which started to push ahead as a feasible financial choice for the island.

Today, Bermuda's global business portfolio incorporates protection and reinsurance, hostage protection, life and annuity protection, protection connected protections, resource the executives, trusts and private customer vehicles, family workplaces, transportation and flight libraries, shipping money and ship the executives, arbitration, recording and innovation, and life sciences. Throughout the years Bermuda has built up a notoriety for development and collaboration in protection and reinsurance. Industry experts together with the administration and the Bermuda Monetary Authority work near find one of a kind answers for customers' needs. Bermuda has a reputation of firsts—the world's first hostage back up plans, the principal overabundance risk bearers, the main property fiasco back up plans and "feline" bonds. With a populace of roughly 65,000 individuals, the island pulls in advanced customers who are intrigued in directing business in an advanced, well-controlled, arrangements situated condition.

**The Bermuda FinTech Strategy**

It is against this financial scenery that Bermuda's FinTech story started when in November 2017, the Government of Bermuda presented a Blockchain Team involving two gatherings who were accused of making an ecosystem dependent on industry information and a comprehension of industry needs, while planning Bermuda to be an innovator in this new mechanical space. The vision was for Bermuda to present noteworthy enactment, expanding on the island's sound notoriety as a world-class controller while understanding the prerequisites of business pioneers in this new innovation.

The Legal and Regulatory Working Group was entrusted with building up a sound, suitable lawful structure to administer items and administrations identified with FinTech. The gathering united universal counselors and industry pioneers with neighborhood controllers, specialized officials, and specialists to ensure the concerns encompassing computerized resources were appropriately tended to through guideline.

Prior to Bermuda, there had been no ward furnished with the combined experience, development, dexterity, and assurance to administratively navigate the universe of advanced resources. This minor island country is pleased to lead the charge, cutting out a complete administrative future for the FinTech industry.

**The Legislative Components**

**Introductory Coin Offering Legislation**

In April 2018, the Government of Bermuda left a mark on the world by drafting and

laying enactment in the House of Parliament that oversees beginning coin contributions (ICOs). Bermuda's Companies Act 1981 and the Limited Liability Company Act 2016 were changed to suit this new class of business. The enactment speaks to a vital foundation of the Bermuda FinTech regulatory biological system.

So as to exploit Bermuda's administrative system, people should initially enroll a Bermuda-based organization or a constrained risk organization (LLC) and be liable to the laws administering business elements in Bermuda. This additionally implies that advantageous proprietors of elements looking to dispatch their ICOs in Bermuda will be checked by the Bermuda Monetary Authority and must meet Bermuda's stringent principles went for limiting dangers identified with cash washing and fear monger financing. Bermuda's business command is consistence, collaboration, and straightforwardness, which means if a genuine worldwide assessment expert solicitations data about the helpful proprietors of an organization, the data will be partaken in understanding with the relevant arrangement.

The enactment likewise presents the base necessities that will be applicable to all ICOs, paying little respect to the rights, usefulness, or highlights of the digital resource offered available to be purchased. Specifically:

• There are necessities for the revelation of data identified with the rights and usefulness of the advanced resources, timetables for any undertaking to be financed with ICO continues, and divulgence of any dangers which may affect the individuals who buy the advanced resources;

• There are explicit necessities for the check of the characters of everybody who buys the computerized resources, including situations where upgraded due persistence is required; and

• To guarantee that buyer personality data is accessible, as required. There are additionally record-keeping necessities for such data.

An application for endorsement to issue an ICO from Bermuda must incorporate a

duplicate of the white paper, and will be liable to examination by a governmentappointed Review Committee made up of lawful, administrative, and innovation experts. Candidates will be advised if extra data is required or on the other hand if extra laws will apply to the proposed issuance. On the off chance that the substance meets the Bermuda Standard, the Government of Bermuda's Ministry of Finance will issue an agree to lead the ICO.

## The Digital Asset Business Act 2018

On Friday, May 11, 2018, two days after the entry of the ICO enactment, the Government of Bermuda postponed the Digital Asset Business Act in the Place of Parliament. The Act has since been passed by the House of Assembly what's more, Bermuda's Upper House, the Senate, and has additionally gotten the important

consent for authorization.

This bit of enactment speaks to a world-first in giving extensive administrative oversight for specialist organizations of advanced resources and related products. With the section of the Digital Asset Business Act, Bermuda has included a basic part to its FinTech methodology, while proceeding to use what is considered the Bermuda Standard. The Digital Asset Business Act, which will be regulated by the Bermuda Money related Authority, is relied upon to fill in as a worldwide model of best practices for guideline of computerized resource specialist organizations. The Act is organized to be generally reliable with Bermuda's administrative methodology for other very directed business exercises, and is designed according to Bermuda's Money Service Business Act 2016, the Insurance Act 1978, and the Investment Business Act 2003. It incorporates a layered permitting structure, against illegal tax avoidance (AML), and antiterrorist Financing (ATF) conventions and prudential prerequisites, customer resource securities, evaluating prerequisites, and authorization measures and powers.

Bermuda perceives that the atmosphere is trying for straightforwardness and the alleviation and counteractive action of budgetary wrongdoings. Similarly as with the ICO legislation, anybody looking for a permit under the Digital Asset Business Act will be required to initially build up a conventional Bermuda organization which will require verifying of the gainful proprietors. The Act explicitly necessitates that organizations have a physical nearness in Bermuda, including a senior delegate who will be in charge of detailing determined data to the Bermuda Money related Authority. Organizations administered under the Act will likewise be subject to various necessities planned to alleviate dangers identified with money related violations, purchaser extortion, showcase control, and dishonest business

rehearses. It is basic that Bermuda's notoriety of being a well-directed jurisdiction is safeguarded, and further upgraded with the nation's entrance into the FinTech space. In that capacity, this exhaustive routine will be actualized in combination with guidelines, codes of training, proclamations of standards, and direction like the administrative structure set up for other budgetary services managed by the Bermuda Monetary Authority.

## Banking Service for FinTech Companies

In the mid year of 2018, Bermuda's Banks and Deposit Companies Act will be changed to make of another class of bank that will give administrations to Bermudabased FinTech organizations. The Bermuda Monetary Authority was counseled what's more, bolsters the changes. The method of reasoning for the presentation is that the FinTech industry's prosperity all around relies upon the capacity of the organizations working in this space to appreciate the vital financial administrations. In different jurisdictions, banking has been the best test and subsequently it must be settled with innovative reasoning and investigated with new choices.

## National E-ID System

The Government of Bermuda is working together with driving technologists to make a national ID plot for individuals and organizations. This will be a stage to help satisfy Know Your Customer (KYC) prerequisites in Bermuda. It will evacuate the requirement for numerous printed copies and written by hand marks. More noteworthy efficiencies will be acknowledged together with business open doors for the government, people, and organizations. It is foreseen that E-ID will turn into a strong worth added option to Bermuda's advanced arms stockpile of business-accommodating arrangements.

## Land Title Registration

In building up the enactment for the FinTech business, Bermuda is creating blockchain arrangements that improve crucial taxpayer supported organizations for the nation's natives. In the primary case, all deeds will be put into an electronic organization, supplanting the present deeds-based framework. With this headway will be the chance to then place the deeds on blockchain, which will render the

records changeless. To encourage imaginative reasoning and inventive arrangements, the government is building up a reason fabricated office for innovation organizations that are domiciled in Bermuda to approach a superior office and bolster services. Organizations will approach a collaborating space, private board room, relax zones, fast web, and attendant services.

## Setting Up Business in Bermuda

Existing help offices have been conveyed to help organizations as they set up their business in Bermuda. The Bermuda Business Development Agency (BDA) is a basic first stop in setting up a business in Bermuda. As an autonomous substance whose command is to help raise Bermuda's profile through targeted business improvement exercises which will help make employments on the island, the BDA gives attendant services to enable universal organizations to set up, migrate, or extend their business in Bermuda. The BDA associates forthcoming organizations to industry experts and

administrative and government authorities, giving choices to corporate administration suppliers and a legitimate help group for the organization enlistment process. The BDA gives a solitary purpose of contact pushing organizations to rapidly and easily build up their essence in Bermuda.

## Outline

Bermuda has joined forces with key industry partners setting up memorandum of understanding which will demonstrate commonly useful in the development of Bermuda's FinTech industry. The organizations that fuse a organization in Bermuda will have progressive enactment to help their improvement and Bermuda will keep on being a hatchery for advances in the business.

In spite of the fact that this minor island a midst the Atlantic is in the beginning times

of its FinTech procedure, Bermuda is guiding the route by reacting rapidly to the market's needs and finding inventive arrangements that will permit FinTech.companies to develop in this beginning industry.

# Conclusion and a Vision for the Future

It is too early right now to say anything decisive for Libra because it has just been announced yet and has about a year to show up in the market is all goes according to the plan. However, once it appears In the market there will still be a lot of challenges which it will have to face to stay relevant such as the big financial institutions like the banks and the government which will try their utmost to limit this currency and impose sanctions on it just like they did for Bitcoin and then comes acceptability that whether the people trust facebook for their monetary transactions and with the security and safety of their money. On the other hand if Libra manages to tackle all of these issues then it can emerge as a Global economy in the World and may play a huge part in shaping and driving the Economy of the World. But still it is too early to come to a final conclusion as this currency is yet to be released and once it hits the market and spends some time there only then we will be able to draw a clear picture of what this currency's impact will be on the World and its Economy.

As for all the kinds of advancements in Bitcoins and Altcoins we have examined all through the book, it will require the responsibility and coordinated effort of governments, innovation firms, and scholarly organizations. This joint effort could prompt supportable monetary development and the advancement of our general society. We are at a crucial point in our history where through advances in technology we have been given both the blessing and the obligation of huge sums of information and the apparatuses to translate and make new boondocks in numerous fields.

Digital money is a standout among the most talked about advances. Innovation has empowered access to make and exchange advanced money and put the chance to take an interest under the control of the general population in a decentralized and not completely regulated way. At its center, government has the obligation to secure its natives, to provide parameters for conduct, and to accommodate their prosperity. In that vein, it is government that records and stores the recordation life's most fundamental and major occasions and events.

Right when a child is born, it is government that gives the birth confirmation. Exactly when that identical tyke transforms into an adult and purchase a home, purchase a vehicle, cast a ticket in choices, and possibly gets hitched, it is government that records and stores that data. Finally, when that proportional individual passes away, it is government that issues a passing verification.